❋ By the rivers of Babylon,
there we sat down, yea, we wept, when we remembered Zion.
We hanged our harps upon the willows. . . .
How shall we sing the Lord's song in a strange land?
❋ Psalms 137

T. S. ELIOT

❁

An Essay on the American Magus

by Marion Montgomery

Published by the University of Georgia Press · *Athens* · 1969

Copyright © 1970 by the University of Georgia Press.

The author and publisher gratefully acknowledge permission
to quote from the following copyrighted material:

T. S. Eliot, Collected Poems: 1909–1962. Copyright 1936 by
Harcourt, Brace & World, Inc.; copyright 1963, 1964, by T. S.
Eliot. Reprinted by permission of Harcourt, Brace & World,
Inc., and Faber & Faber, Ltd.

The text of this book was set in 10/13 Caledonia by Graphic
Services, Inc., York Pa. The book was printed on 70# Mohawk
Superfine Text by Braun-Brumfield, Inc., Ann Arbor, and bound
with Interlaken cloth at the Dekker Bindery, Grand Rapids.
Designed by Fred Thompson.

Library of Congress catalogue card number: 76–90551
Standard Book Number: 8203–0232–5

To the Memory of Donald Davidson

Preface

✤ This essay is deliberately digressive, exploratory. It is a reading whose primary interest is the evolution of Eliot's commitment to Christianity as reflected in his poetry. Since it is not a formal, comprehensive reading of all his work, I have documented sparingly, trusting that the interested reader will recognize my indebtedness to many critics of Eliot, an indebtedness I have chosen to pay through echo and allusion rather than by the encumbrance of more formal acknowledgments. From Eliot's work I have depended primarily on his *Collected Poems: 1909–1962* (Harcourt, Brace & World, Inc., 1962). The following works have been particularly helpful as points of departure in the introductory sections: T. E. Hulme, "Romanticism and Classicism," *Speculations* (Harcourt, Brace & Company, 1924), J. B. Bury, *The Idea of Progress: an Inquiry into Its Origins and Growth* (Dover Publications, Inc., 1955), R. G. Collingwood, *The Idea of History* (Oxford University Press, 1956), Frank Kermode, *Romantic Image* (Random House, Inc., 1964), and Robert Langbaum, *The Poetry of Experience: the Dramatic Monologue in Modern Literary Tradition* (W. W. Norton and Company, Inc., 1963).

I am indebted in a more personal way to a number of persons, and in particular to the late Donald Davidson, who read an early draft and commented on it with that generosity of spirit and of intelligence known to so many. I should also like to record here my gratitude to the following among my colleagues, so that they may share responsibility for encouraging me, to Charles Beaumont, Ernest Bufkin, Calvin Brown, James Colvert, George Core,

William Davidson, William Free, Edward Krickel, Warren Leamon, Robert McRorie, Boyd McWhorter, John Talmadge, Robert West. Being so many, they will not find that burden intolerable I trust.

.

Marion Montgomery

Spring 1969
Crawford, Georgia

> . . . To apprehend
> The point of intersection of the timeless
> With time, is an occupation for the saint—
> No occupation either, but something given
> And taken, in a lifetime's death in love,
> Ardour and selflessness and self-surrender.
>
> *The Dry Salvages*

Prologue

✿ Eliot is our great intellectual poet. He is also, perhaps, our greatest romantic poet. He considered himself our classical poet. Confusion confounded. It was as romantic that many received him initially, abandoning him when he seemed to turn preciously intellectual, thus turning the poem back to the academy, as William Carlos Williams lamented. That the early Eliot was romantic in one respect at least, he himself remembers in his essay on Dante in 1929. There, speaking of a "prejudice," he recalls as "natural to one of my generation," he describes it as "the prejudice that poetry not only must be found *through* suffering but can find its material only *in* suffering. Everything else was cheerfulness, optimism, and hopefulness; and those words stood for a great deal of what one hated in the nineteenth century." The alienated poet, clasping his misery in defiance of Browning or Tennyson, was true descendant of Keats and Shelley. But looking with older eyes, Eliot says, "The eighteenth and nineteenth centuries knew nothing" of our own "prejudice against beatitude as material for poetry," though "even Shelley . . . , the one English poet of the nineteenth century who could even have begun to follow [Dante's] footsteps, was able to enounce the proposition that our sweetest songs are those which sing of saddest thought. The early work of Dante might confirm Shelley; the *Paradiso* provides the counterpart, though a different counterpart from the philosophy of Browning." Thus Eliot, reflecting on the nineteenth century in its relation to the poets of his generation, himself now far advanced in following Dante's footsteps. If people as diverse as Wallace Stevens and Karl Shapiro were put off by Eliot as high-toned old Christian lady (shades of

1

John Milton), the academy tended to welcome him as religious romantic. For Eliot as Christian royalist is less an embarrassment in this perspective than a rich mind of paradox, excellent subject for clinical exegesis.

As one looks at the body of his poetry, which reflects the development of his position, one sees him at once acknowledging his romanticism, while showing it inadequate. What I shall want to consider in the body of this essay is a developing realization in the poems themselves of the incompleteness of both emotional and intellectual response to the world, whose point of coincidence with the mind is the image. His poetry comes to insist upon an enlargement of awareness by grace, even as Dante's emotional and intellectual awareness comes to be enlarged at a point of ascent in his poetry by the mystery of Beatrice, the God-bearing image.

But as a preliminary to my argument that imagery constitutes Eliot's Beatrice, it might be well to make somewhat more clear the nature of that romanticism Eliot acknowledged, to see something of the question of imagery as it began to haunt Eliot with its psychological and metaphysical questions. *Imagiste* was the new name for poet as Eliot makes his way into print for the first time, with V. S. Flint and Ezra Pound defining the term vehemently so as to recruit anti-nineteenth century activist poets to their cause. But the best point of departure for my purposes is T. E. Hulme, founder of the "Poet's Club" and first of the new imagist poets. Hulme, who was to die in World War I in France, was never close personally to Eliot. His temperament and appetites must in any event have set them apart. But they are generally taken to be close companions in critical theory, Eliot himself praising Hulme as "the critical conscience of his generation." That Hulme professed himself Christian long before Eliot came to do so is, I suppose, one of the reasons emphasis is given to Hulme's influence on Eliot. In addition, they are in common agreement that *classicism* is superior to *romanticism,* as F. O. Matthiessen long ago pointed out. Hulme's distinction between those terms, made aggressively in his "Reflections on Violence," is particularly acceptable to Eliot by the time he begins to echo Lancelot Andrews in his poetry. The classical mind, Hulme argues, carries a conviction "that man is by nature bad or limited, and can consequently only accomplish anything of value by discipline, ethical, heroic, or political. In other words, it believes in Original Sin." Romanticism, on the other hand, embraces "all who do not believe in the Fall of Man." And in "Romanticism and Classicism" he attacks the Rousseauistic doctrine of infinite progress, seeing that doctrine as a delusion, a violation of reality itself with dire implications to the poet who embraces it.

It is beyond this point of agreement that Eliot and Hulme begin to diverge, more markedly than generally supposed. For in his concern for a neoclassical revival in poetry, Hulme attacks the relevance of metaphysics to aesthetics. Quoting Ruskin at length on the "imagination" and its solemn, serious requirements, he concludes that Ruskin "wants to deduce his opinion like his master, Coleridge, from some fixed principle which can be found by metaphysics." When Eliot attacks romanticism in "Tradition and the Individual Talent," he pursues a line parallel to Hulme's assault upon the romantic imagination, but he concentrates on the creative process as requiring a dissociation within the poet, a schizophrenic dissociation of the poet as "maker" from the poet as man. "The point of view which I am struggling to attack is perhaps related to the metaphysical theory of the substantial unity of the soul: for my meaning is, that the poet has, not a 'personality' to express, but a particular medium, which is only a medium and not a personality, in which impressions and experiences combine in peculiar and unexpected ways." In his attack upon Wordsworth's argument that the poet is a man speaking to men, and that the heart of poetry lies in emotion recollected in tranquility, Eliot brings his attack to bear upon the scholastic conception of the "substantial unity of the soul," an attack he withdraws

3

from not so much through his interest in St. Thomas Aquinas as through the mysticism of St. John of the Cross.

From such correspondences between the views of Hulme and Eliot on the nature of classicism, it is possible to exaggerate their kinship. One must look more closely at the implications of Hulme's arguments, developed out of his belief that the image is "the very essence of an intuitive language." Indeed, Hulme is in this statement closer in his beliefs to his fellow Imagist Ezra Pound than to Eliot, as indicated by Pound's emphasis on the virtues of the Chinese written character and his insistence that poetry's root and blossom are both limited to the finite world. To make the most of image, Hulme announces *fancy* as the "necessary weapon of the classical school" of poetry he sees emerging about him. And he insists emphatically that the poet must address particular things in the world with "zest." But the zest he calls for one is soon to find more abundant in the poetry of Wallace Stevens than in Eliot. Indeed, though Stevens calls it *imagination,* his "necessary angel" is far more compatible to Hulme's "fancy" expressing the poet's zest for the things of the world than to Eliot's "impersonality" of the poet with its emotional detachment. It is through a zest for things, Hulme argued, that the poet discovers the multiplicity of metaphor through which alone the language of poetry can be made precise.

To Hulme the enemy of poetic precision, and a sure sign of romanticism in poetry, is the constant intrusion of "infinity," with its attendant seriousness and solemnity that denies beauty to the "small, dry things" of nature. Imagism itself is not sufficient to the most effective poetry, such attempts at making the word correspond to the thing as we find in the best of William Carlos Williams. Metaphor is finally called for. Yet the overlaying of images, the making of metaphor, must not tempt the poet to assume that a metaphor implies either a transcendent reality or a possible future utopian brotherhood. To Hulme the romantic's attraction to "infinity" on the one hand and to the doctrine of progress on the other are both seductions of the mind away from the concrete reality of the world. On the one hand, "You might say . . . that the whole of the romantic attitude seems to crystalise in verse round metaphors of flight." On the other, the root of romanticism is the belief that man is "an infinite reservoir of possibilities; and if you can so rearrange society by the destruction of oppressive order then these possibilities will have a chance and you will get Progress." Reading Hulme's words, one remembers at once illustrations of those metaphors of flight which abound in nineteenth-century poetry through skylarks, nightingales, mockingbirds, and hermit thrush. And one thinks as well of the nineteenth-century optimism which was as repugnant to Eliot as to Hulme, the cultural humanism of Matthew Arnold or Tennyson, the democratic optimism of Walt Whitman.

One must consider that, although sparrows in the gutters and hermit thrush among the pines are inadequate to the beatitude Eliot seeks, there is nevertheless a constant flight underway by the personae of his poetry, up to that late affirmation of a still point. It is a flight from particular things in which Hulme expected the poet to find beauty. There is an uneasiness in Eliot's personae as they find themselves in the presence of the "thousand sordid images" of which their souls are constituted in the poetry, whether "a broken spring in a factory yard" or the other "withered stumps of time" one encounters in a luxurious London room. Hulme argues that flight, celebrated by the romantic poet as the possible achievement of the imagination, is a pursuit of the transcendent. Consequently the romantic poet is unable "to admit the existence of beauty without the infinite being in some way or another dragged in." But the belief that the metaphor is a valid instrument toward transcendental truth, and that consequently the poet's imaginative powers are equal in importance to the scientist's empirical analysis of the world itself, is doomed. It is doomed, to Hulme's thinking, because the romantic misunderstands the nature of metaphor. For metaphor involves a transfer of one term, which the poet may

5

share with the scientist, to a second term as its predicate, an action which necessarily violates predication itself. To Hulme such distortion of the world through language, an action of the fancy, "is a compromise for a language of intuition which would hand over sensations bodily." Since "images in verse are . . . the very essence of an intuitive language," metaphor—the distortion of images by fancy—enlivens sense response. Multiple imagery is triangulation brought to bear upon the senses. But it does not reveal hidden truth. Metaphor, one might say, is a species of pungent sauces such as Gerontion no longer finds adequate to arouse sensations.

There is then in Eliot one aspect of romanticism which Hulme repeatedly attacks, an inclination to the infinite, the transcendent. Hulme wished to oppose that conception of nature which the romantic poet struggled to maintain in the face of his attraction to the contradictory doctrine of Progress: namely the belief that there is a fundamental unity in the world beneath appearances which justifies metaphor as a legitimate instrument toward an abiding, abstract truth. What Hulme argues for. to the contrary, on behalf of his neo-classical poet, is a chaos of the world, within which the poet's mind may operate for its own pleasure as an agent. His fascination with Bergson leads him to take the natural world as at once destructive of the mind's order and at the same time constituting the materials out of which order is possible. Because of his fallen nature, man is himself a part of that disorder, so that it is "only by tradition and organization that anything decent can be got out of him." There is an eighteenth-century optimism hovering about Hulme's confidence in the mind's power, much as there is about Pound's. He asserts an intellectual independence of the world more than the spiritual independence which Eliot finally comes to accept. Thus Hulme can, in the realm of poetry, transpose Wordsworth's "similitude in dissimilitude" from the realm of imagination to that of fancy. Likeness in unlike things is an operation upon the world by the poet's mind dependable only so long as there is a "concentrated state of mind" which

6

maintains a "grip over oneself." Fancy is "superior to imagination" in that there is a holding back by the poet "even in the most imaginative flights." Such a poet saves himself that romantic agony born of the failure to hold back, a failure which makes a Keats ask, following his seduction by his deceiving self, "Do I wake or sleep?"

What Hulme almost says, but does not quite come to, is that the romantic split between the imagination and fancy—out of Coleridge's definitions of the terms—is a recognition by the romantic of his failure. It is an attempt to cope with that fallibility in man which is counter to his Rousseauistic belief in man's infinite capabilities within the world. "Romanticism . . . is split religion." Coleridge's fancy is the romantic's substitute for the doctrine of Original Sin, dangerous in the romantic's view to the cause of both his poetry and Progress. To the contrary, Hulme argues: fancy is superior to the romantic's concept of the imagination because it makes possible the celebration of the poet's zest for things, regardless of the profundity of the particular thing. Thus it is the poet may find beauty "in small, dry things." Fancy allows for a recurrence of joy independent of any metaphysics that would insist upon an orderly account of the multiplicity of things. The memory of things recaptures the zest without the sad telling of nature's sad decay, for the poet is relieved by fancy of a responsibility to nature's mortalities.

We may observe, as Eliot increasingly did, that in the absence of a metaphysics, the worship of things for themselves becomes the sign of a new romanticism. Keats's things of nature—urn or nightingale—suggest the infinite through the decay of the things themselves. His use of nature is replaced by things considered in themselves infinite. The poet's responsibility then becomes the infinite proliferation of imagistic assertions of things. All the poet's poems are one motion of this assertion, an assertion without direction beyond the act of imaging itself. It is a change in our poetry to be remarked in Wallace Stevens' joyful construction of

7

a pineapple as well as in Allen Ginsberg's endless celebrations of the self as God.

Hulme's classicism is a more appropriate anticipation of Wallace Stevens than of Eliot. In opposing the temptation of the romantic poet to see a presence of the transcendental in the concrete particular, he argues metaphor in the same sense Stevens argues it: metaphor is the instrument for the naming of an infinite sequence of *resemblances* anchored in the real world. "Metaphors of a Magnifico" and "The Idea of Order at Key West" affirm a zest compatible to Hulme's requirements more surely than Eliot's affirmation of the Word within the word. Eliot must finally affirm an order beneath the appearance of disorder, an order to which he found the language of poetry appropriate.

We should notice that Eliot's early poetry does indeed seem an illustration of those uses of fancy which Hulme calls for when he says "We shall not get any new efflorescence of verse until we get a new technique, a new convention, to turn ourselves loose in." But one cannot escape a different holding back in that poetry from the restraint characterized by Hulme as through the mind's being concentrated and in control of itself. Nor is this holding back in the early poetry to be identified finally with that disengagement from the world which Eliot argues for in "Tradition and the Individual Talent." "There is a great deal, in the writing of poetry, which must be conscious and deliberate. . . . Poetry is not a turning loose of emotion, but an escape from emotion; it is not the expression of personality, but an escape from personality." In *Prufrock and Other Observations* and *Poems, 1920* there is a holding back which I take to be out of a fear, not simply of the romantic's indulgence of personality, but a fear of the very technique of the poems themselves, the uses in them of Hulme's fancy. For fancy may prove misleading, even when controlled by the mind, since in some way not yet discovered by Eliot there is a distortion of the very things of nature represented with such imagistic effectiveness in his early poetry. It is a holding back that makes the bolder Pound reflect on "Grishkin's photo with the feeling that Mr. Eliot may have missed something, after all." It is a holding back that made Wallace Stevens, among others, feel Eliot as a "negative force." For certainly the zest Hulme calls for is missing in the early Eliot, a zest one remarks abundantly in Pound and Williams and Stevens. In setting himself apart from Eliot, Wallace Stevens makes a distinction appropriate to *Paterson* and to much of the Cantos no less than to his own "Whole of Harmonium": "For my own part I like to live in a classic atmosphere, full of my own gods and to be true to them until I have some better authority than a merely contrary opinion for not being true to them."

While Eliot rejects their view of infinite progress in the world, he is reluctant to abandon the possibility of transcendental meaning implicit in nature. Into the general chaos of images of which Eliot's early poetry is constituted there begins to intrude a new source of order which would ultimately require a rejection of fancy as the poet's chief weapon. Pointedly, in "What the Thunder Said," we abandon that journey through the streets and alleys of that early poetry, including the journey in *The Waste Land* itself as ordered by London streets and the course of the Thames from west of London, through the city to the coast at Margate. That journey in the world of things and unhappy people is abandoned for high and arid hills that are of a world less anchored by the particulars of London and the English countryside than by Dante's ascent among shades in Purgatory. The hermit thrush is abandoned for a pursuit of the "city over the mountains." The emptiness of history with its "voices singing out of empty cisterns and exhausted wells" is put behind. The quest is not now so much through images, though they abound, nor by an imagined flight of skylark or nightingale. The movement now is through "the awful daring of a moment's surrender" which is beyond the restraints of prudence. The restraint, the holding back, begins to fade as there enters increasingly into Eliot's poetry an awareness of order larger than the poet's mind. It is an awareness calling for a surrender that Eliot worked hard to come by in his skeptical age, and it cost him, he finally says, "no less than everything."

But it gained for him the world of nature seen in a new way, a newness measured by the distance between the restraint in the presence of a seemingly sordid world in that early poetry to a zestful love of the same world which emerges in the *Four Quartets*. The change is in Eliot, for it is the same world in both instances. He has arrived where he started but knows the place "for the first time." The bones out of rat's alley have begun to sing after "twenty years largely wasted." And we may notice, as we look and listen with Eliot's new eyes, that even Gerontion's hapless attempts to "excite the membrane . . . with pungent sauces" has given way so that "smell renews the salt savour of the sandy earth."

ii

❀ Given a world in which an absence of community with his audience handicaps the poet, a progress in his poetry can hardly depend upon systems of thought or established techniques of narration. Eliot discovers system and technique through the exploration of his own spiritual inadequacies, most disturbingly present in the difficulty of accepting the immediate world. That disturbed awareness in the poet, caused by the uneasy intrusion of the external world, affects the use of image by such a later romantic as Eliot. For the "objective correlative" which an image establishes also allows an imposition of the indefinable "feelings" upon an image, as in the famous instance of Prufrock's evening as a patient etherized upon a table or as in the imagery of "Preludes" about which feeling curls. Let me propose that Eliot's early use of image is very much in accord with the implications of Wordsworth's argument that the emotions give importance to a situation or action rather than the other way around.* Thus it is that one may most fruitfully consider Eliot's complexities through a change in his use of the image. One might say that it is the image itself that proves to be Eliot's Beatrice. Or more accurately, one might say that the image becomes as Beatrice's eyes to Dante, in which Eliot comes to see the marvelous changing of nature—the desert—yielding the hidden nature of the Word.

* On this point I have argued elsewhere, considering the meaning Eliot supplies to such terms as *feeling*, which he advances against Wordsworth's *emotion*. See my "Eliot, Wordsworth, and the Problem of Personal Emotion in the Poet," *Southern Humanities Review*, II (1968), 185–197. See also my "Emotion Recollected in Tranquility: Wordsworth's Legacy to Eliot, Joyce, and Hemingway," forthcoming in the *Southern Review*.

Intellectual consent, Eliot comes to tell us, is early; commitment more inclusive than the intellectual sometimes follows. He is talking about a movement of the mind such as Coleridge might call the willing suspension of disbelief. But it is an intellectual commitment in the interest of seeing into what Wordsworth called "the life of things" (including, in Eliot's instance, the image itself); it is not a suspension on such an elementary level as that required in our allowing a mythical element to function dramatically in one's reading of the *Inferno*. It is rather a point Eliot is defining in the sequence of psychological process leading to a spiritual rebirth. Intellectual consent follows that stage he describes in his essay on Bradley (1927) in which "skepticism and disillusion are . . . useful equipment for religious understanding." It is also a stage preceding that condition of the mind which can at last see its relation to the world from a still point more radical than that enjoyed by the "enthusiastic mediaevalists" of the nineteenth century, whom Eliot alludes to disparagingly. For there is too much suggestion of the Walter Mitty or Miniver Cheevy in those optimistic enthusiasts such as Tennyson and Browning. Even the more careful analysis of the self as it relates to the world, advanced by Matthew Arnold, bears in it a fixing of the "self" through the formulated phrase that does not go to the soul of the problem. "The distinction," Eliot says, "is not between a 'private self' and a 'public self' or a 'higher self,' it is between the individual as himself and no more, a mere numbered atom, and the individual in communion with God."

Such is the argument one encounters in Eliot's recollections of his spiritual progress, instances of which may be multiplied out of those critical pieces in which the art or argument of a Dante or Lancelot Andrews or Francis Herbert Bradley is the immediate correlative. But the arguments are dramatically present in the play of imagery in his own poetry. It is an argument made in summary in the *Four Quartets*, and the point of that argument is especially emphatic in the "lifetime's death in love" of the initial quartet which leads on to that life in love of the final quartet. *Burnt Norton* is for Eliot an examination of that death in life which the memory contains, a recollection in tranquility of experiences analogous to Wordsworth's recalled in "Tintern Abbey," through an awareness larger than the commitment of the intellect. The detail, summoned from the past by memory and rationalized out of Heraclitus, cannot adequately account for one aspect of that recollection, the intimations hovering about a concrete experience of some reality larger than the child could comprehend or the man account for philosophically or psychologically: the roses in Eliot's early garden "had the look of flowers that are looked at." Wordsworth would have recognized the feelings in that line at once. What he might not have understood, as Eliot had not in his "Preludes," is that there is a third presence in the scene. Yet the "feeling" in the child's blood that his eyes are not the only eyes on which the rose depends for its existence is not finally an embuing of nature with a soul, or rather an enlivening of image with the seer's eyes, and the romantic poet's anthropomorphic address to the world. For one to conclude from *Burnt Norton* and its epigraph that ". . . the appositeness of the epigraph from Heraclitus and to the pattern of *Four Quartets* is good evidence of the continuity of Eliot's thought through all its transformations" is to overlook a change in that continuity, in which Heraclitus becomes Christianized as it were. Eliot's quest is constant; his understanding of the particular points at which he stands in "Preludes" and *Burnt Norton* are very different.

    Burnt Norton is concerned with reflecting the light of a new position upon the old. Eliot, one might say, has stood with Wordsworth on the banks of the Wye. (One notices how close geographically Burnt Norton is to Wordsworth's ruins.) What Eliot has seen in his "Preludes" is not a little line of sportive wood run wild, but "such a vision of the street / As the street hardly understands." As if recollecting the "Preludes," Eliot describes the child's intimation of a calling, mistaken to be the bird's, just beyond the first gate, and then "hidden in the shrubbery," an "unseen eyebeam crossed" with the child's own seeing. A difference in details between Eliot and Wordsworth, but not a difference in the relationship of the poet to the external world in "Preludes" and in "Tintern Abbey." For "Preludes" is a city figuring of "Tintern Abbey" in which the poet acknowledges being

> . . . moved by fancies that are curled
> Around those images, and cling:
> The notion of some infinitely gentle
> Infinitely suffering thing.

In *Burnt Norton* Eliot has come to confront that experience (less deliberately detached from his own "personality" than is true in "Preludes") with a rationale more firmly asserted than Wordsworth manages in his *Prelude,* or in the "Intimations Ode" for that matter. In *Burnt Norton* images are touched by a reality larger than an empirical psychology or a logically-adumbrated phenomenology can explain, a reality which humankind cannot bear very much of. Eliot has openly come to affirm a light which is so overpowering as to seem, in the ordinary sense, not light but darkness. That dark beam of the timeless touches time, not in a vague dispersal as with Wordsworth's light that never was on land or sea. It touches a still point in the individual awareness, with an immortal wound through which alone Eliot is able to escape the old romantic dilemma of history's relation to the individual: the deceptively temporal imaging of eternity in finite awareness through which

> Time past and time future
> What might have been and what has been
> Point to one end, which is always present.

That romantic awareness of time's involutions of awareness itself, which is the source of those fancies curled about images, is insufficient to him, for in such a seeing one must conclude that "All time is unredeemable." This still point of awareness is the still point of the romantic mind in despair, a moment of epiphany, transient and illusory, followed by implication or direct statement that the awareness itself is threatened by time's annihilation. It is the fear expressed in Keats's and Wordsworth's and Shelley's separate versions of the mind's questioning of reality: Do I wake or sleep?

But it is at this still point also that Eliot finds the dark ray touching individual awareness. The roses that have the look of flowers that are looked at may be looked at with a light which has made the child's eyes other than they were. Beatrice is no longer across the stream of forgetfulness; the eyes absent to the voices in "The Hollow Men" are now the eyes of the beholder himself, eyes from which the veils of time are lifted. Grace allows a seeing out upon the images. A new contingency, independent of memory, is realized, and the child is transformed into the seer in a way quite different from Wordsworth's dream in the "Intimations Ode." The notion of "some infinitely gentle, / Infinitely suffering thing" becomes immediate and particular: in time, yet transforming the individual awareness so that it may transcend time. That earlier presence which hovers vaguely in the rose garden, seemingly separate from the child, becomes resident in the mature mind. When one comes to see *himself* as an image of God, as Eliot does, he sees images out of nature in quite a different light.

Eliot overcomes to his own satisfaction the threat of the image's illusion, that threat which led Wordsworth to question the validity of awareness itself and Keats to lament those fancies that moved him. Thus is he finally reconciled to his tradition by moving beyond it, which is to say that he is finally reconciled to the terror and pity of himself as a center held in that time which is eternally unredeemed. (This early condition of the individual soul is analogous to that of the unredeemed soul in Dante's Hell which so painfully bears the past and future as its present.) With the dark ray of grace the individual awareness rises to behold eternity buried deeper in the awareness than history is buried in it, touched both by growing garlics in the *now* and buried sapphires from the *past.* Time's residue so clots the bedded axletree that it must be uncovered. In which process one sees the lowly, even offensive, herb bearing in it that old tree out of Eden. The awareness begins to hear that "trilling wire" which "sings below inveterate scars." It begins to hear more deeply than the history manifest in the individual. Forgotten wars are reconciled to the present as they are not in "Gerontion." Finally a new awareness moves in a new light "above the moving trees," a movement quite other than the goings-on of things in nature which we call history. In *Burnt Norton* Eliot is affirming a transcendence which neither Keats's nightingale nor Yeats's golden bird could accomplish. From that new elevation of awareness which is "not out of time," nature is reconciled to its implications of time unredeemed, and derivatively, time is reconciled to nature's images. Boarhound and boar in the fierce forest are reconciled to their configurations in the stars by an imagination which does not violate nature through its transnatural desires. It is an imagination which does not see the star as "Nature's sleepless Eremite" or constellations as "huge cloudy symbols of a high romance." It is not a Keatsian flight of fancy.

But neither does Eliot celebrate a mighty being that is awake in nature as Wordsworth does in recalling his state of suspension in nature. Like Plato, Wordsworth describes as lost and longed for a condition in nature in which

> . . . the breath of this corporeal frame
> And even the motion of our human blood
> Almost suspended, we are laid asleep
> In body, and become a living soul. . . .

Such is the dimension of Wordsworth's still point, but it is different from Eliot's version of that experience in which one is

> Neither flesh nor fleshless;
> Neither from nor towards; at the still point, there the dance is,

> But neither arrest nor movement. And do not call it fixity,
> Where past and future are gathered.

As similar as these still points in Wordsworth and Eliot might at first seem, Wordsworth's is an attempt to reconcile the present moment to past moments, and both to future moments. Wordsworth is finally occupying a temporary point which he abandons, moving back down into the world. His concern is principally for a moral relationship of nature to "a living soul" which has not managed to transcend time any more than Keats does in pursuing his nightingale. He does not quite conclude, as does Eliot, that "to be conscious is not to be in time." Time indeed drags him back into the world, and he addresses Dorothy on the contingent future, not on the timeless as it affects the contingent. Wordsworth's having seen in his youth what Eliot objectifies as happening to the "dry pool," promises only to be a way of bearing "too much reality" to the older Wordsworth, when reality is seen in temporal terms only. Memory is a means of revisiting the Wye when solitude, fear, pain, sorrow become too much for one. Hence the temptation to return to the Wye or to the garden:

> Go, said the bird, for the leaves were full of children,
> Hidden excitedly, containing their laughter.

With the urging of bird call, one looks

> . . . down into the drained pool.
> Dry pool, dry concrete, brown edged,
> And the pool was filled with water out of sunlight,
> And the lotus rose, quietly, quietly,
> The surface glittered out of heart of light,
> And they were behind us, reflected in the pool.

The "they," recollections in tranquility of past selves, sustain the illusional waters of the sun only momently. The dry concrete images are finally only dry concrete images. Eliot's thrush is as deceptive as Keats's nightingale or Wordsworth's inland murmur or smoke or sportive wood run wild.

The fancies that curl about images in "Preludes" have proved insufficient in themselves. Still we must notice that Eliot is unhappy with romanticism because he was an unhappy romantic. He has stood where Wordsworth and Keats and Shelley have stood, and he speaks as one who knows that country. They are an undeniable part of what he knows. That he carried the *Divine Comedy* about with him as religiously as Alexander carried the *Iliad* we remember. What we tend to overlook is that it was Shelley's and Tennyson's poems that interested the young Eliot.

iii

❀ Robert Langbaum, in *The Poetry of Experience,* describes the romantic poet's significant contribution as a dramatization of an epiphany in which a reader participates by seeing with the eyes of the poet at the moment of the poem.

> But the content and meaning of what he sees has existence and validity only within the limiting conditions of his gaze, which is why any idea we may abstract from the poem for general application is problematical.

In effect, then, a reader participates in the romantic poem as in a closet drama, except that the poem is so restricted as to be most effective when there is only the reader enacting the poem. The willing suspension of disbelief in his enactment of the poem does not so much require a disinterestedness as it requires a temporary subjective immersion. To use a term currently applied to recent attempts to enlarge the audience of the romantic experience, the romantic poem is to the reader a private "happening." That experience and our present public happenings differ in relation to reader or audience from the traditional relationship of drama to audience in that there are no inherent or external controls upon the "happening" which allow a disinterested perspective. Oedipus' experience as we see him destroyed is to Oedipus himself a private happening also, though he is moved by a public concern. But the presence in the audience's mind of the full myth, the presence on stage of Jocasta, Creon, Tiresias, makes a response possible which is larger than our simply participating in the emotional reactions of Oedipus to his developing circumstances. The participation in an epiphany whose fruit is only emotional response is not finally satisfying, since the very emotions aroused are not finally "purged." [*] A sense of history, willy nilly, is brought to bear upon the romantic epiphany, either a sense of the general movement of western civilization or the general movement toward maturity out of adolescence in the individual. To the extent that a sense of history is added to one's experience of the romantic epiphany, to that extent one is better able to relieve those emotional pressures aroused by the romantic poem's subjectiveness. This necessity of bringing the external to bear upon the objective existence of the poem is part of the difficulty of the new critical approach to the romantic poem, though if one were to make a statistical study of the problem, I suspect he would find the typical new critic devoting more attention to romantic epiphanies than to any other aspect of our literature. For here in particular there is room for an emphasis upon the ironies of subjectivity as examined analytically. What the strict new critical approach does not allow is a relating of the significance of that literary epiphany to real life, a concern I shall argue which becomes increasingly insistent in Eliot, one of the principal fathers of the new criticism.

The problem of the epiphany in romanticism, with which Wordsworth and Keats for instance struggle, is that it involves one in an infinite regression or progression. So long as that epiphany is an element in the simple love lyric, as in Waller's "Go, Lovely Rose," or Donne's more complicated delights, the pleasures of subjective submergence are hardly formidable. But when the whole burden of metaphysical system bears down upon an isolated epiphany, its inadequacy to that burden becomes more and more apparent. As with Keats's Cortez, one stands on each peak with a "wild surmise" of new worlds only now imagined. As with Tennyson's Ulysses, one stands in the momentary arch through

[*] I have argued the limitation of romantic tragedy as opposed to classic tragedy such as Eliot's in an essay, "In Pursuit of Melpomene," forthcoming in the *Arlington Quarterly* for Winter 1970.

which he gazes upon a constantly receding world. The journey, whether that of Keats's knight at arms or Wordsworth's poet in the *Prelude*, has more concern for and emphasis upon the temporary points occupied than in the direction or the end. Langbaum comments that the "limits of the narrative or drama of experience [the romantic] are not logical but naturalistic." It is so of the romantic's ode or ballad as well, for escape of time through a naturalistic imaging of epiphany can only be temporary. That "escape" of nature is unsupported by a metaphysics whose foundations are more profound than emotional response to or reaction against the naturalistic. Keats inevitably wakes on the cold hill side, and Wordsworth comes to question the reality of awareness itself.[*]

The epiphany, which one might call in Frost's words "a momentary stay against confusion," is the romantic poet's contribution to the new doctrine of Progress out of the Enlightenment. But it is an expense of spirit too large for the artist to bear. It threatens the possibility of form itself, limiting form by the moment at which one stands on a particular peak, aware of peak and ocean. It is an effect in art partially out of the development of empirical science, to which Wordsworth had advised the poet to provide the first and last of all knowledge by accompanying that science at every step. In accompanying science step by step, however, the poet found increasingly that imagination itself was victim to naturalistic authoritarianism. Out of empirical science grows the new religion of Progress, which defines a sequence of its own epiphanies in time, but to an end which proved to be increasingly that Utopian materialism already manifest to Wordsworth in the corruptions of altar, sword, and pen. The fruits of that dream we know most immediately in our own alienated age perhaps in refrigerators and television sets and cars, whose virtues are deliberately momentary: that is, this year's model is regularly superseded

[*] See my argument on this point in "Wordsworth and the Ghost of the Mind: The Seductions of Metaphor," *Georgia Review*, XXIII (1969), 169–182.

before All Saints' Day. Thence also the aspirations of political or social man: he would stand upon the latest progressive peak as well as ride the latest car or rocket. The poet is consumed by the fallout in his art: the latest in form. But to Eliot "to make it new" becomes a valid cry in proportion as the *it* is of an abiding significance. (It is precisely on the nature of the *it*, for instance, that Pound and Eliot diverge.) Eliot comes to believe that, if there can be no journey's end which is impregnable to time, one is committed to a finite movement in time which denies any relevance of art to life save only the fading moment of awareness. The romantic's alienation is not elected; it is determined by laws of naturalism to which not marble nor the gilded monuments of princes is exempt.

Such, in part, is the background to Eliot's emerging disaffection with romanticism, through which disaffection he came to recognize the modern world's *low dream* as he calls it in his essay on Dante. The world of the thousand lost golf balls is also the world of the wild-eyed man in the latest model car on the super-highway. It is the world of the beat poet with his diarrhea of epiphanies sprawling on the page. The father of all these, *in perpetua*, is the god Progress. (And how ironic all these children as father to their god, engaged in a private, negative anthropomorphism: without hope out of desire, without form out of despair.)

Langbaum defines the poetry of the romantic as the "poetry of experience." It "communicates not as truth but experience, making its circumstance ambiguously objective in order to make it emphatically someone's experience." It is, then, an escape from the terrors of relative truth. But an Eliot cannot be satisfied in his appetite for an absolute truth by the subjective, private synthesis, those movements of the mind which must inevitably reach a terrifying conclusion: absolute alienation. This condition of awareness in the romantic is quite separate from the silence which spiritual mysticism leads one to, a state in which one gives the self as the lamp gives light. Not as one projects image to mirror independent of light.

The development of Eliot's imagery from his early to his late poetry is such as to show an increasing awareness of this distinction. For Eliot works away from the poet's projection of himself into an object so that he may say something to himself, the characteristic romantic use of image which both Langbaum and Frank Kermode explore. In projecting an image of himself which he then engages in dialogue, the romantic poet seeks to overcome his sense of alienation but rather commits himself to an illusion. For the procedure is a technical maneuver mistaken for fundamental insight into reality. It is as if the poet should himself mistake the pretended address of the rose as a literal communication with the rose. The failure of the romantic's address to image is evidenced finally by the poet's being unable to connect anything with anything with any abiding confidence. He is, once more, finally reduced to the question, *Do I wake or dream?* For always the dream is incompatible to the world in which he dreams.

The experience of the reader in the poem of reality, through his suspension of disbelief, is such as to leave him, after his ambiguous experience, with the feeling that he has experienced "someone's experience." The experience of the poet is similar. For to write a new poem requires of the poet a suspension of disbelief as the necessary "poetic faith" as Coleridge says. It is a mark of the separateness of his poems, for he is engaged upon that series of infinite epiphanies as individual discoveries of the self to the self. Such is a primary limitation of the lyric, which viewed historically shows a tendency toward emergence into drama, as in the emergence of tragedy out of Dionysiac hymns, the development of Shakespeare toward his tragedies, of Shelley toward *The Cenci*. And it is in the development of Eliot from "Prufrock" to *The Cocktail Party*. In such serious attempts upon the epiphany, each poem, as Eliot says in *Little Gidding*, is a new beginning, a new step. Each alone moves. But seen as a movement of the poet—that is, the poems seen as a body of work—separate steps become walking. The question of sameness becomes insistent.

But the sameness of the *it* in poems made separately, if the *it* has not deepened or grown, puts excessive pressures upon form to disguise that sameness. Form becomes its own end. Finally, one has quite enough odes from Keats. Or finally, one recognizes the shift of form in the body of Joyce's work as forced by his static *it*. The sophisticated devices of *Finnegans Wake* obscure the basically similar romantic walking which Joyce earlier assumed in *Chamber Music*. And even within individual poems the reader is called upon for separate suspensions of disbelief. Consider Shelley's "Ode to the West Wind," for instance, as it is paralleled by another romantic poem, Shakespeare's Sonnet 73. There is, in Shelley's ode, a repetition distinguished by separateness of detail, but no movement or development which enlarges significantly toward the poem's final section, which attempts to function analogously to Shakespeare's couplet. There is a desperate serious-ness in Shelley's incantation of images in defense of his alienation; but there is no convincing resolution of that desperation in the final cry of spring imminent. For at the end Shelley resorts to dead metaphor such as Shakespeare employs more effectively in his sonnet. Shakespeare's metaphors are more effective precisely because, as T. E. Hulme might argue, the fancy is controlled by the poet's self-control; there is a detachment from the self-pity which the sonnet indulges, as there is not in Shelley's self-indul-gence. A significant difference in the two poets' use of images, then, lies in an awareness in Sonnet 73 that the appeal to the emotions through image is not an appeal with fundamental validity. Finally, Sonnet 73 is a game the poet plays with his voice and wit and not an attempt at a profound address of the self or of the world at large. Shakespeare moves on to his plays.

The separateness of Keats's Odes, the separateness of the portions of Shelley's "Ode to the West Wind," one encounters in the *Excursion*, the *Prelude*. The effect of the totality of works, observed with detachment, is of having traveled a mountain range of a particular sameness, having emerged upon no significant plains, nor risen to any significant height. One feels compelled to suspend not disbelief, but belief, and substitute for it the illusion of experience, the recognition of which requirement affects even the poet—Keats despairs in nature, Wordsworth of the validity of mind itself. The romantic lyric is a part of a larger drama in the poet, whose passion tempts him to a belief in the illusional. It is in the light of this failure in the romantic poet that Eliot criticizes the romantic mind rather severely in his prose, while himself discovering a progress out of romanticism through his own poetry. Langbaum, after an analysis of Keats's "Ode to the Nightingale," asks, "Does the poem then deny itself? What is left us in the end? The thing we are left with is the thing the observer is left with—a total movement of soul, a step forward in self-articulation." But toward what end of any abiding comfort to the soul? For, as Eliot says, in addressing the romantic's dilemma in *East Coker:*

> The poetry does not matter.
> It was not (to start again) what one had expected.

And in *Little Gidding:*

> . . . last year's words belong to last year's language
> And next year's words await another voice.

Keats's soul, and Wordsworth's, are drawn to last moment's or last year's experience as the matter of this moment's poem. Caught in an infinite repetition of steps, distinguished by the accidents of time and circumstance, the poet pursues similitude with a desperateness heightened by the terrors of dissimilitude, the effective agent of alienation. Such is the concomitant in poetry to the new history (which R. G. Collingwood examines in *The Idea of History*) in which for instance the cycles of the mediaevalist so attractive to the romantic mind, become lost in the welter of heightened particulars. The attempt is to project a *line* of movement out of the dance Eliot finds at the still point. Wars of the spirit or of nations are unlike, goes the modernist argument, for one is in different terms from the other. The particulars of difference are emphasized. Weapons change, dress changes—that is, *images* change. But one has an illusion of a progress or of lyrical steps that become a walking, while losing an awareness of fundamental similitudes that go deeper than the surfaces of metaphor or history. It is the romantic as victim of time that engages Eliot, more sympathetically than the romantic himself usually realizes, as witnessed by attacks upon Eliot from the romantic's position these past twenty years. It is to the problem of escaping time's despotism that he increasingly addresses himself, seeking to come to terms with history, searching for its chains within his own blood that the chains may be loosened. The search moves him from an initial low innocence he shares with the modern world, through the accidents of his being in a particular time, to a high innocence he finds implicit in the nature of his being.

He comes finally to believe that a dark ray of grace touches the individual awareness so that the individual awareness may be at once in time and out of time. Otherwise the Heraclitean siftings would be unbearable, as indeed they are to the romantic. Particular moments in alleys or rose gardens of the world become particular in the memory insofar as the moment can be placed in time. But the significance is not that of the moment's rest from movement, as he says in *Dry Salvages,* for "time is no healer: the patient is no longer there." Every attempt at containing the moment is "a wholly new start" (*East Coker*), since it is always an attempt to move out of time, an attempt in Eliot's view to hear and say the Word. But that very attempt endangers, not the Word, but the listener, the seer:

> The Word in the desert
> Is most attacked by voices of temptation,
> The drying shadow in the funeral dance,
> The loud lament of the disconsolate chimera.
> (*Burnt Norton*)

In short, the Word is most attacked by the romantic image which is nevertheless the desert's victim. "Desire itself," the spring of words, "is movement / Not in itself desirable" (*Burnt Norton*). The hearing, the saying of the Word within the word—which is at the center of the multitudinouse detail of the desert—is a said silence, a paradoxical phrase, like St. John's dark light.° For the significant movement of awareness is not on the plane of time, in which words or things have their being, but tangent to it, in which awareness discovers itself in time but recognizes itself also as out of a mysterious silence that precedes those contingencies of time that burden the memory. Memory is a danger to awareness since memory is history's child, however much Wordsworth would press it back to a Platonic recollection of knowledge preceding time. Yet out of the mystery of history's silence, one must attempt to escape by articulating tradition in its temporal dimension. In that articulation the awareness may move toward a wisdom of silence, not lineally in the flow of time—the moving tree of *Burnt Norton*, the moving waters of *Dry Salvages*, the waste words of

° Etienne Gilson (in *The Spirit of Thomism*, 1966) remarks: "That one does not see any light, may be a fact; to infer from it that there is no light, *is a non sequitur.*" The comment is in a chapter, "A Metaphysics of the Name of God," which seems to me highly pertinent to the history of Eliot's pursuit of the Word, from his Bradleyan studies to his more comfortable assurance in the *Four Quartets.* Gilson explicates Saint Thomas' argument for the *Being* at the center of *being,* or in Eliot's late phrasing of the idea, "the Word in the desert." He proceeds from Saint Thomas' argument that the act of being has no quiddity of its own "precisely because it does not belong in the order of essence." *Existence*, the act of being, is separate from the existing of a *particular being;* that separate act of being is signified by a judgment: namely, that *existence* is the common principle of all existing things. "That *whatness* [*ens*] of things [*res*] differs according to their respective natures, but concerning their *thatness* [*esse*], only one of two things can be done—it can be affirmed or denied." The act of existence, which is common to all things, is "not [itself] a being but rather is that which makes such and such a thing to be a being." "All the other beings are essences, or substances that *have* their respective acts of being; but their universal cause is not an essence having such an act, it *is* that very act." The argument that *esse* is a name of God is then related to scripture in which existence is affirmed as the name of God: *Qui est* (Exodus 3:14). Eliot, underlining the highest attribute of man, intellectual substance, chooses his phrase out of the New Testament: the Word in the desert.

Little Gidding. More importantly it is a movement Heraclitus suggests in his "way up and way down" as disengaged from the temporal—without direction, since the way is in a dimension other than time's. The "way" Eliot would seem to recognize as the dark stair which St. John affirms as opening upon a dimension of the soul beyond curved space, that stair which Eliot is striving to accept more largely than with intellectual consent, as in *Ash Wednesday.*

The isolation of the soul, which is inevitable to this movement, does not put the soul at distance from the kind, for it has learned "to care and not to care." That is, it can give itself to the building of the temple out of its knowledge of the temple's inevitable decay. Such is Eliot's classical assurance, which does not allow lament for the fate of rocks nor for the urns or gilded monuments of princes or the common kind. For romantic images, made as projections of the self, are hostages to destructive time, disconsolate chimeras mourned as companions by Langbaum's "poet of experience." The soul, seeing with that dark light too strong for the world's eyes, sees monuments, even those of this year's poems, as insufficient, though an inevitable corollary to its existence in time. The poet's images are recognized as being in a language itself infected by time's slow virus and are therefore the most subtle entrapment of the poet's awareness by the world. Thus words, like stone images, must be willed victims, and the "classical" awareness such as that of the late Eliot willingly dedicates those words as sacrifice.

> For last year's words belong to last year's language
> And next year's words await another voice.
> (Little Gidding)

Only the Word, always in the desert, is unaffected, whose fullest articulation is the active silence of assent. Thus it is that every poem that is right is an epitaph of a failure of the word (the poet), unable to speak the Word, that is, unable to become himself an adequate image of that silent Yes, which in *Little Gidding* is named the Calling, by which we know Eliot means Christ.

Eliot's poetry then moves toward a *quietness*, like that of steady breathing. The stasis the artist comes to, all passion spent in him, is silence. When he goes on living, we may make the mistake of thinking of him as written out, implying a kind of decay. In fact he may have achieved an eminence of being never before realized in his life. We want somehow to have St. Thomas' final silence explained in terms of a stroke, the body's decay that drags down a great mind. But that may be only because we find such explanations easier to understand than the mystery of wisdom, to speak nothing of the mystery of Grace. Thus wisdom might well caution us against seeing a progressive weakening in Eliot's poetry in the first place, and in the second of ascribing as cause of degeneration his Christian affirmation, which our age wants characterized as a last and intolerable infirmity in any noble mind that comes to that affirmation.

❀ Eliot's symbols differ from Dante's, Robert Langbaum has suggested, because they "put forth an atmosphere of unlimited meaningfulness." They seem rather to put forth diverse intimations of one meaning, whose center was difficult for Eliot to locate. For, though in his criticism he is repeatedly concerned for the poet's control of his material, and particularly his control of "objects, a situation, a chain of events," he finds that control not absolutely resident in the poet's power. That is, Eliot is moved by intimations larger than his intellectual awareness can reduce to words, while for some time he is committed to words by a belief in their efficacy, a common bond with Pound. One must, on this point, however, make a distinction between the rationalization Eliot provides to the one center early in his career and that which he provides in his final poetry. This distinction is one J. Hillis Miller too much subdues in over-emphasizing "the continuity of Eliot's thought." For the still point of Bradleyan psychology, reflected in "The Love Song of J. Alfred Prufrock," is very unlike the mystical still point reflected in *Burnt Norton*. In Prufrock the still point establishes, not an "individual in communion with God" as Eliot is prepared to describe it in 1927, but a stage of arrested development of the spirit, in which the world is kept at bay by the intellect through images infused (and so distorted) by the feelings. Those feelings allow the intellect to compose arms "braceleted and white and bare," but cannot accommodate the image's coming alive: the "light brown hair" is cause for panic, until the intellect regains control of images by composing "Arms that lie along the table, or wrap about a shawl." The distance between the two poems is the distance between an

uneasy recognition of an inadequate *state of being* and the realization of the profundity of *being* itself in communion with God.

For that reason, to see in Eliot's poetry as a whole a conclusion
that "the mirroring ego has swallowed up the world and everything
exists inside the looking glass" is to distort Eliot's poetry. For it
is not true to the poetry to see the same use of image in "Prufrock"
and *Burnt Norton.* The coincidence of subject and object, whose
representation in the poem is what one might call voiced image,
is everywhere accompanied in that early poetry by pathos, the
sad awareness of an inadequacy in the Bradleyan monochism.
Eliot's early exploration of Bradley's "monistic metaphysics" is an
attempt to substantiate a condition of psychological being prior
to self-awareness in which there is an obliteration of distinction
between the subject and object, as in the speaker-evening images
with which "Prufrock" opens. Such monistic existence comes to
be interrupted by the individual awareness, through which there
comes to be the dualism of the *self* and the *other.* In his dissertation,
then, one sees Eliot in pursuit of the epistemological problem that
so plagues Wordsworth. Eliot argues that "Experience . . . both
begins and ends in something which is not conscious." We recall
Wordsworth in pursuit of such unself-awareness in "Tintern
Abbey," the *Prelude,* and "The Intimations Ode." Once consciousness of self is introduced, the duality leads on to a confusion in
which appearance is taken for reality, for, says Eliot, "the ideal
and the real, the mental and the non-mental, the active and the
passive . . . are terms which apply only to *appearance.*" So long
as both subject and object are inseparable, through an absence of
self-awareness, being is monistic. One is happily unreflective in
his environment, being thereby closer to the pair of ragged claws
Prufrock envies.

Eliot, in the final paragraph of the essay appended to his
dissertation ("Leibniz' Monads and Bradley's Centers"), for all his
intellectual assent, asserts Bradley's "monadism" only as impecca-
ble in its technical excellence. He concludes, "I am not sure that

the ultimate puzzle is any more frankly faced, or that divine intervention plays any smaller part." Bradley, finally, has "the melancholy grace, the languid mastery, of the late product." Eliot recognizes a logical trap in Bradley's monism, I think, without being as yet prepared to confront the problem adequately. For the system requires a negative assertion—the non-existence of self-awareness—which, even if granted as possible to the individual being, yet prevents a convincing comprehension of what that state is like. By the act of attempting to confront the problem, one prevents the possibility of an experience ending "in something which is not conscious." For such an end is an *unnameable* state of being. Both Eliot and Wordsworth address themselves to that condition; Eliot for instance dramatizes the intrusion of self-awareness upon Prufrock's state of mind as the cause of pathos, even as happens unintentionally to Wordsworth in "Tintern Abbey." In respect to the individual being, existence is not absolutely prior to state of existence, since existences precede any individual existence. That is, history itself prevents that initial "something which is not conscious," as well as a final, longed-for condition in history. To name that state even vaguely is to step into dualism.

When Eliot argues from the philosophers, rather than from recollections in nature as does Wordsworth, that *one* is necessary so that we may say *one-in-two-parts*, he has taken a position separate from both alternatives, but it is a position no more valid philosophically than saying the opposite: that *two* (or the "many") exist that *one* may be said. Eliot's Bradleyan explication of experience attempts, through a more technical and abstract diction, to find a source in the mind to explain what Wordsworth calls "feelings of unremembered pleasure," an authority for that "serene and blessed mood" in which self-awareness seems dissolved and one is so laid asleep in nature as to become "a living soul." The old philosophical dilemma inherited from the *Parmenides* is presented as a "late product" of the mind; that is, philosophy is now crossed by empiricism turned from nature upon the mind, out of which rises the science of the mind, psychology. Yet an empirical approach to awareness—the careful examination of subject-object relationship—is always open to objection for the simple reason that our "scientific" approach to mind, which has such fascinating results in recent biology, is necessarily through awareness itself. It is more difficult to characterize the emergence of self-awareness, obviously, than to backtrack biological emergence into the secrets of DNA. Yet even in such study—biology, crossed by physics—one is forced to acknowledge an influence upon the object from the observation itself, whether one attempt to observe in the child a monistic being before its fall into consciousness or observe particles of matter. As a further complication, biochemistry since Eliot's Bradleyan phase, is increasingly moved to postulate mind in all organic matter, even if in a closed teleological sense such as that argued by Edmund W. Sinnott in *Matter, Mind and Man.* And the question of whether some level of awareness is inherent in all matter has been arrestingly raised by Teilhard de Chardin in *The Phenomenon of Man.*

C. S. Lewis uses an argument analogous to Eliot's Bradleyan thesis, in *The Problem of Pain,* but Lewis's is a spiritual *monism* posited as peculiar to the prelapsarian state of man, with the coming to self-awareness as the cause of the fall from that innocence. Lewis's is a way of looking at man's history, generally and individually, which Eliot himself comes more and more to accept,° so that he is led to distinguish high innocence and low innocence, before and after the fall, and argue a recovery possible only through a movement of the mind larger than the limits of the intellect. The monism of Bradleyan psychology gives way to the Monism of Orthodoxy, to that Calling of the Word in which self-awareness

° The two men move toward orthodoxy concurrently, Lewis giving a particular history of his own development in his autobiography, whose title is from Wordsworth, *Surprised by Joy;* the title celebrates a moment of grace in nature which turned Lewis toward orthodox belief.

is obliterated in a silence which does not deny individual consciousness to the self but is rather a state of unself-aware awareness.

Perhaps some light on his changed monism is intended by Eliot in his figure, in *Burnt Norton*, of garlic and sapphire clotting the bedded axel-tree. It is as if, in his figure, Eliot is looking back upon Bradley with images out of Frazer, but images changed by a new sense of the still point. The tree as an axis linking diverse worlds pervades mythology, as Eliot could not but know. It symbolizes variously the linking of three worlds—earth, upper world, heaven; it signifies human nature. It represents also the Cross, and so comes to represent the center of the cosmos, an axis or still point of those revolving worlds Eliot had such difficulty reconciling to the "ancient women / Gathering fuel in vacant lots" in "Preludes." The psychological estate of monism, preceding self-awareness, has given way to a conception in which individual awareness is involved by a new dualism to be accounted for out of an initial state of innocence. The Tree of Life and the tree of the knowledge of good and evil are not seen as *two* until the latter is experienced. The Tree of Life is hidden from Adam till after his experience of knowledge's tree. Eliot was, of course, acutely aware also of that elaborate ritual in Dante's Eden in which the two trees are brought together in that rich pageantry he praises in his essay on Dante. In speaking of that element of the *Purgatorio*, he says, "It belongs to the world of what I call the *high dream*, and the modern world seems capable only of the *low dream*." Each man his own Adam, one comes to that tree through which his own image is transformed as he recognizes Christ as the Still Point, the Axis of the universe holding all together in a monism that can account for the relation of all things (the "many") to Itself, whether those things be multiple myths or images. The image is no longer an aspect of individual awareness reflecting upon the awareness. Christ is Eliot's cosmological answer to Copernicus and Galileo. But He is also Eliot's answer to the problem of the dissociation of individual sensibility whose history lies in that post-Renascence decay of metaphysics which left modern man incapable of accounting for his own awareness. When awareness cannot be satisfactorily accounted for, neither can the image's relation to awareness.

In one respect Eliot's Bradleyan thesis seems an attempt at explaining the romantic's use of image. That is, one may consider the romantic's use of image as an attempt to recapture the monistic state of experience in which self-awareness is obliterated. Frank Kermode, in his *Romantic Image*, explores Stephen Dedalus' concept of image as common to the romantics, a concept which Stephen emphasizes as governed by *concretion, precision, oneness.* That concept embodies two beliefs, Kermode argues: a belief "in the Image as a radiant truth out of space and time, and in the necessary isolation or estrangement of men who can perceive it." The observation is certainly appropriate to Stephen, as witnessed by his Keatsian flights of imagination through the bird imagery he dwells upon and by his final retreat into a communication with himself, through the diary pages which conclude *The Portrait of an Artist as a Young Man.* The radiant truth is to Stephen finally an aesthetic stasis in which sensibilities dissolve into the mind's images, a stasis analogous to Eliot's Bradleyan postulate of stasis before self-awareness fractures an experience. But ours is an ironic view of Stephen's attempt, in which we depend upon our knowledge that the image, as separate from awareness, is individual and fallible, an argument at least as old as Socrates. Stephen's faith can lead him only to talk with himself, for such a stasis is a private and incommunicable state of mind. Joyce is forced to give us an oblique and ironic view of Stephen, experiencing his stasis, a view further complicated by Joyce's own mind of which one has also an oblique and ironic view in its relation to Stephen's. It is questionable that one experiences any image as Stephen does, which difficulty has led to a naturalistic approach to Joyce and his work by some critics. "Joyce's Dublin" is catalogued in an attempt to give substance for an emotional epiphany in Joyce's reader, as if that procedure were appropriate to that fiction, a substitute for myth, and so allow the effects of reversal and recognition one experiences in *Oedipus the King*.

What we must finally conclude, however, is that to the extent to which we can see Stephen, and through him the images he struggles with, we can be sure only that something happens—Stephen does react to images. He then rationalizes that reaction. The monism of Stephen's experience, which Joyce so carefully manipulates, is finally out of that absolute control of point of view, which is Joyce's supreme achievement as craftsman. Joyce's achievement is that his work is not seriously violated by the external world, whether by the world of biographical facts in Joyce or in Stephen's auditor, the reader. The work then has those virtues Keats attempts to make absolute in his Grecian urn. Joyce's Portrait, however, is of a limited effect in that Stephen's portrait does not touch the reader's awareness in a fundamental way, as Oedipus or Dante's Pilgrim or Lear do. When Eliot expresses himself as unhappy with aspects of Joyce's style, it is with an aspect of Joyce's style akin to that he objects to in Milton. For Eliot's dissatisfaction is with a dissociation of sensibility through which the image comes to be used in a romantic mode to create an illusion of a community of experience between the reader and the agent.

Isolation and estrangement are difficult to bear. Joyce, the most powerful of our romantic minds, could not himself bear it without complaining. What wonder then that Eliot seeks a stasis in a truth larger than a monistic psychology, applied to image, could manage. He moves on from "The Love Song of J. Alfred Prufrock," as Wordsworth does from "Tintern Abbey." For Eliot's early use of image is dictated by an entrapment of mind in nature; that is, the romantic projection of image in words is a pursuit of a spiritual stasis dictated to by the limits of time. Most usually the pursuit is of a time past, through recollection out of a desire for tranquility. That attempt inadequate, Eliot began to look for a radiant truth indifferent to time, a movement in answer to that

Calling which he, like Wordsworth, has intimations of early. It is a truth, he concludes in the *Quartets*, which is not ultimately dependent upon the inherent weakness of language's attempt to justify or affirm the existence of one's awareness. Eliot's argument now finds the image's radiance residing neither in its name, the word, nor simply in the external thing, nor in the experience of the observer confronted by an object whose name is a secondary concern to the confrontation. The radiance of the experience results from a presence independent of the presence of an awareness in nature. A separate order of existence enters upon the experience, the mystery of grace.°

In contrast Keats's poetry bears the poet's desire for a monistic state of the mind-object relationship, as when the poet attempts to fade away into the nightingale's song. But subjectivity is the

---

° Gilson, in "The Master Plan of Creation" (*The Spirit of Thomism*), pursues Saint Thomas' argument of man as an image of God: intellectual substance as a resemblance of its transcendental cause. That intellectual substance, which distinguishes man as an existence, is provided with two external aids to the perfection of its being: nature and grace. Its faculties of reason and faith respond to those aids: reason moves inductively, through a recognition of a hierarchy of ordered causes in nature, toward a knowledge of God; faith moves deductively out of revelation to affirm a knowledge provided by the agency of grace. As Gilson summarizes the relationship: "The philosopher ascends from the knowledge of nature to the knowledge of God, the theologian descends from the perfections of God to those of his effects." But, he adds, "since that twofold movement takes place within one and the same mind, the philosopher and the theologian are bound to meet." Again, "although philosophy ascends to the knowledge of God through creatures while sacred doctrine grounded in faith descends from God to man by the divine revelation, *the way up and the way down are the same.*" "Philosophy, which is about nature, establishes the possibility of what revelation promises; revelation brings to man the certitude that the obscure aspirations of his nature will be fulfilled in eternity." Eliot in his early years may be said to exercise what Saint Thomas calls "a natural inclination toward his [man's] ultimate end." But he is sometime coming to accept St. Thomas' argument that man cannot attain his ultimate end "by natural means but by grace only, and this is because of that very end." That acceptance is indicated by the epigraphs from Heraclitus which preface *Burnt Norton*. The first confronts that human arrogance which violates the Word; the second announces the twofold way, which grace enters upon: (1) "Although the Law of Reason (logos) is common, the majority of people live as though they had an understanding (wisdom) of their own." (2) "The way upward and downward are one and the same."

curse Keats cannot overcome, for it is inevitably fostered by individual fallibility which loses sight of "ideal and real, the mental and the non-mental, the active and the passive" as "terms which apply only to *appearance*." We see the workings of delusion if we take the following statement by Keats and relate it to the best of his poetry. "The Imagination," he says, "may be compared with Adam's dream—he awoke and found it true." The analogy is self-deceptive, for in it Keats attempts to equate John Keats's dream (his imaginings) to Adam's dream. Keats's poems belie the assertion, acknowledging the imagination as invariably a "deceiving elf" leading one to an awakening on a cold hill side that one can only hope, out of despair, possibly illusion. One must not overlook in Keats the personal immediacy of his concerns with the imagination. Keats cannot maintain Joyce's detachment as artist. He is not concerned with literary technique or with the artistic process when he speaks of pecking gravel through the sparrow or of shouting with Achilles in the trenches. He is talking about an awareness of his particular, private existence which he records in words that betray him. Still, to him that existence is paramount, not its record. In *Hyperion* he speaks of attempting to recover "the large utterance of the early gods" to save himself, not in order that he might make poetry, as Joyce might be said to use Homer to make *Ulysses.* Keats seeks a stasis which Kermode describes as *"un-dissociated,* mythopoeic,"* a phrase which suggests Keats's concern with Eliot's own "dissociation of sensibilities." The enemy of Keats's possible joy is, of course, self-awareness, which inevitably leads to analysis, and so to the conclusion that he is separate and alone. That is the base note of Keats's melancholy.

Eliot of course comes to see in Dante a way out of the romantic's entrapment by the image. Dante's usage is in sharp contrast to Keats's. One has, in Keats's vision of Moneta's face in *Hyperion,* a reflection of horror and a fascination with it at once like that in Dante's confrontation with Satan in Hell and Dante's encounter with Beatrice on Purgatory. Keats's poet is fascinated by her eyes, but not as Dante with Beatrice's. For the fascination (which prevents flight as if the poet is confronted by Medusa) is with the hopelessness. There is no getting past Moneta, as past Satan. Keats's joy is in despair, once more a moment of the crushed grape on fine palate. It is as if Dante, viewing Satan, should then discover not the prospect of the mountain lying beyond, but an enthralling vision of Ante-Hell. It is to the Keatsian hero a feeling of "What 'tis to die and live again" before a literal death, but the living again is that which one knows in the rich decay of nature on that inevitable cold hill side. Dante's prospect on Hell, through which he puts pity and terror behind him, affirms a High Justice. Keats's vision leaves a bitter-sweet taste of injustice, through which the poet "venoms all his days, / Bearing more woes than all his sins deserve." Keats has looked into the void, from which no recovery of the soul is possible to him, for there is no way of seeing which is not dictated by the void itself. The griffon he sees in Moneta's eyes is himself, receding and wasting, changing between hope and despair. From such a vision no spiritual development is possible.

I think we will do no great violence to Eliot by suggesting that Keats's experience and Dante's experience are both a part of what Eliot knows, not simply from his analysis of the poets' works, but most directly through the agony of his own poems. To a considerable extent the *Four Quartets* acknowledge his early romanticism and his kinship to those poets he tends to attack in his prose: Wordsworth, Shelley, Keats. He sees emerging out of his own private struggle the recognition of a center of experience which is of universal significance, though words are finally inadequate to that significance. "The poetry does not matter" finally, at least not in the way it at first seemed to matter when he was struggling to complete *The Waste Land* and save his sanity thereby. "It was not . . . what one had expected." Yet it was through poetry that Eliot came to see "a limited value / In the knowledge derived from experience," and to affirm Dante's vision as applicable not only to the "middle of the way / But all the way" since all of life is spent "in a dark wood" we call the world, in which grace alone lights that dark way sufficient to the toil required. It is to some detail of the struggle along that way, as reflected in the imagery of Eliot's poems and the modulation of the voice one hears speaking those images, that I now turn.

I

❀ Eliot said, in his recollections of Pound in *Poetry* for September 1946, that at the turn of the century there was little in contemporary or recent poetry for the young poet to turn to. He is very particular in citing Browning as more confusing than helpful. And yet it seems reasonably clear from our vantage point, looking at the development in Eliot and Pound and at modern American poetry in general, that Browning showed a way out of the limited personal confessional that the romantic tended toward, however much Browning seemed to have failed in Eliot's eyes. The critical emphasis upon influences on Eliot and Pound has tended to be upon their fascination with foreign literatures, for instance upon Eliot's interest in French poets from Baudelaire to Valéry. Eliot himself encouraged such a particular interest not only through his poems that quote or allude to those French moderns or his early poems actually written in French, but also through the attention he pays the French in his essays.

One need not set aside, indeed must not set aside, the importance of Laforgue or Valéry to Eliot. We have come to see, as much through Eliot's work as through his argument, that close attention to a separate language is a discipline of the mind in that it requires of the mind a particular attention to syntax, diction, music. But a separate language is also a protection, a defense to the poet. It is worth considering whether such influences as the French poets on Eliot are not primarily that they help Eliot come to terms with his own romanticism. Keats and Shelley and Wordsworth prove themselves closer to Eliot's youth than he felt himself comfortable with. Laforgue's sardonic irony is less disquieting than Keats's direct melancholy. It isn't until after *Ash*

Wednesday that he can admit himself as "possibly too romantic" in his taste.

The influences upon Eliot's technique, exercised by the symbolist poets in particular, are accidental to his substance, though startling enough to be arresting in this "new poetry" which one encounters in *Prufrock and Other Observations*. The interests of Eliot's technique, indeed, were sufficiently refreshing in a dull poetic time to put off that necessary reckoning with his true center. Actually that center was more startling to his contemporaries than his technique. Williams sounded the alarm after *The Waste Land*, and even Pound chided "Reverend Eliot" in the *Cantos*. More recently Karl Shapiro, in his anti-academic phase celebrated by *In Defense of Ignorance*, chides us for not taking into our critical account of Eliot's poetry and critical influence the spiritual center of Eliot's concern. To Shapiro, Eliot is dangerously subversive precisely because he is a religious poet.

The art which Eliot learned from the French romantics (though not entirely from them, as we shall presently consider) seems now rather curiously necessary to those anti-Eliot critics who seem to react against his poetry to the degree that they recognize its tendency toward Christian traditionalism. They are likely to depend more heavily upon those extremists of the imagination, Verlaine and Rimbaud, than on Baudelaire, who has become respectable in the academy, or Corbière, whose mind is that of the classicist as defined by Eliot. One notices, for instance, that Shapiro (in his angry manifesto against Eliot and Pound) praises Verlaine and Rembrandt and then follows them into the labyrinth of excessive romanticism in *The Bourgeois Poet*, trying to force accident to be substance. Eliot never allowed himself the luxury of that confusion. Though he did not at first find a suitable relationship between the universal and the concrete which afforded soul's peace or a comfortableness about aesthetic argument, he was reluctant to seize upon the one or the other with the desperation, say, that led Shapiro to seize Whitman and elevate him to the rank of Apollo—or perhaps I should rather say Dionysus. This uncertainty in the early Eliot accounts for his reservations about Milton on the one hand and about Poe or Keats or Yeats on the other. The reservations are rather self-consciously restricted to poetics, early and late. But particularly in the early Eliot one notices a care to avoid the rock upon which he came finally to rest. It was as if Eliot were indeed intent upon turning poetry back to the classroom, as William Carlos Williams accused him of having accomplished with *The Waste Land.*

Still, this "academic" concern is not the heart of his matter. He dedicates *On Poetry and Poets* to Valéry, a collection of essays which includes a late revisiting of Milton in which he explains why "the study of his verse might at last be of benefit to poets." And meanwhile Valéry has proved insufficient to Eliot's concerns, as he argues in a lecture after the *Four Quartets* are behind him, and with *The Cocktail Party* just ahead of him.

II

✥ In that lecture, "From Poe to Valéry" (1948), one notices an insistence on Eliot's part that the failure of the poetry stretching from the American poet to Eliot's friend is that it allows no growth of mind and spirit. What Eliot is unhappy about finally is that one has in such poetry an elevation of adolescence as the supreme theme. Hemingway, during these years marked by Eliot's development from *Prufrock and Other Observations* to *Ash Wednesday,* is wrestling with the same problem in different medium. *The Sun Also Rises* has as its final epiphany Jake Barnes's acceptance of his own arrested development, which is expressed in the last line of the novel. Eliot was bothered by this curse upon American literature of our century, the cause of the exodus by many of the famous expatriates: the childish awareness of childishness. When Huck Finn can't "lite out" for the West any longer, he heads East, about the time of World War I. After World War II, of course, it becomes possible for him to lite out in whatever direction he will, preferably in no direction, though San Francisco was for a brief confused moment a point of reference. One may pursue this spectacle of adolescent flight in the fictions or the lives of F. Scott Fitzgerald, Thomas Wolfe, Hemingway, W. C. Williams. It is in the fake primitivism of Gertrude Stein and in Amy Lowell's love affair with Imagery.

Henry James, Eliot, Pound are different from these in that they three are not satisfied merely by the awareness of arrested development—either as it exists in our culture or in themselves. All three seem older, more remote to us, in consequence of this element of their awareness. Indeed Conrad seems much closer to us than James and we almost forget that Eliot and Pound are contemporaries of Frost and Stevens. Of course the three were restless, a fact which allies them in one sense with the "younger" expatriates. (W. C. Williams was older than Eliot or Pound, as were both Frost and Stevens.) But that kinship of restlessness does not lead them into the Pyrenees on fishing trips, nor into the withdrawal of a Gertrude Stein into a tower where she can be both the dragon who besieges and the princess besieged, nor into other attempts at recollecting bright, innocent childhood as if it never went away. One must say, whatever else might be said, that James, Eliot, and Pound wrestled larger giants than their own private wounded selves. The artist of adolescence, one should notice—such people as those I have named among those pilgrimaging to Paris (and it is a sign of difference that James, Eliot, and for a time Pound settled in London)—the artist of adolescence seems constantly calling attention to his honesty, an act which immediately calls honesty into question, as a woman's insistence that she is a lady raises doubt. For neither honesty nor ladyliness is properly self-defended.

We have then to look elsewhere than to the expatriates or to the French poets for Eliot's kinships. *The Four Quartets* indicate the direction our search should take, since those poems celebrate the culmination of the journey of magus Eliot, rather than a new voyage entirely, as Pound attempted in *Hugh Selwyn Mauberley* upon discovering London unsuited to his dream of the ideal city. Eliot's is initially a movement backward into time, not a shift of place, in pursuit of an escape of time and place; or rather his is an attempt at an *accommodation* of the spirit to time and place. Again, one should note the difference in Hemingway's concern for the *moment,* as compared to Eliot's, his attempt to recreate "the way it really *was*" as a denial of time. The personal moment is divorced from time through willful self-memory in which any place will do, whether Michigan or Paris or Africa. Hemingway's pretense at an interest in history is suspect. He scarcely gets beyond Napoleon or his generals, and they are likely to be statues against which he leans in a Paris park in the 1920s. (See his conversation on "Mike" Ney in *A Moveable Feast*.) Nature itself is a moment of sensation, with as little implication beyond the sensual response as the will can prevent. Indeed, Hemingway is constantly being frightened by the shadow of implication. Thought is the worst hell possible, since thought focuses on the fleetingness of the moment. The trouble with Fitzgerald, according to Hemingway in *A Moveable Feast*, is that he thinks: "Later he became conscious of his damaged wings and of their construction and learned to think and could not fly any more because the love of flight was gone and he could only remember when it had been effortless." (The intrusion of thought into the flow of language is precisely the objection of W. C. Williams to Pound's *Draft of XXX Cantos* in his "Excerpts from a Critical Sketch.")

In contrast, Eliot, himself uneasy in his approach to history, nevertheless pursues history in all its horrors of time. He does so as the possible way toward the timeless as Baudelaire pursues the horror of the particular as a negative, a correspondence, to the universal. Eliot isn't intent upon a boundless moment of illusion, as is Keats. Nor is he able to content himself with Frost's subjunctive view of man's role in time. Frost, we notice, plays "suppose," proceeds "as if" what seems to be is more than a seeming. So doing, Frost escapes being overwhelmed by uncertainty, by the complication of illusion and reality, as were Wordsworth, Keats, and Frost's friend Robinson. Nor does Frost seize upon one illusion to make it eternal, as Hemingway seized upon the private moment; he sees a variety of possibilities, in the process of which he presents a multiplicity whose center of control is a skepticism, sometimes generous and friendly, sometimes impish, sometimes waspish. But the limitations are such upon the subjunctive that, though they allow a considerable lyric range in a mind such as Frost's, a mind such as Eliot's could only have been defeated by the attempt. What Eliot required, as he came to see more clearly, was a center from which he could blossom, a center which could reconcile the details of time, the almost infinite moments, to the timelessness. If Milton's dogmatic verse may be a threat to the poets who come after him, Frost's view of the impossibilities of knowing are a threat to soul's rest, as Yvor Winters charges in "The Spiritual Drifter as Poet."

Frost could say with a mixture of seriousness and mischief,

> We dance in a circle and suppose
> While the secret sits in the middle and knows.

But Eliot must come to rest at the still point of the circle. He might find helpful to his cause the study of the accidents of poetry such as those appropriated from the French, but what he was most intent upon discovering was an abiding reality that must be approached through time and place, the two limits upon a mortal's quest. It is this necessity in him that makes him a romantic, but he has a degree of perseverance and a firmness of mind which finally, it seems to me, leads him beyond that romantic poet who is skillfully disguised in *Prufrock and Other Observations*. We see that this is so in Eliot by the time we come to the final of the *Four Quartets:*

> The moment of the rose and the moment of the yew-tree
> Are of equal duration. A people without history
> Is not redeemed from time, for history is a pattern
> Of timeless moments. So, while the light fails
> On a winter's afternoon, in a secluded chapel
> History is now and England.

The rose of eternity—Dante's multifoliate rose that has plagued Eliot since long before *The Hollow Men*—and the yew-tree of time—the church's earthly life in the country churchyards of England, stretching roots to the dead kings and queens of history and toward all above, to all below and between. Thus one has in him a separation by his discursive mind that made for Eliot a more tenable vision than Stephen Dedalus' confusion of yew and rose in that prolonged pursuit of the "place of green roses." Yew and rose, for Eliot, are reconciled within the individual soul when it has come to terms with its own existence. For Eliot, the reconciliation comes after long journeys of the spirit. It leads him finally to that assertion that "history is now and England," in which the *now* is the timeless moment, *England* being history's moments of time which the *now* encloses. Not just the particular disengaged morning sunrise in Pamplona with the bulls rushing into the arena. The reconciliation comes too late in Eliot for him to celebrate the joy of dappled things, as Hopkins could do, though there are some inklings of joy in the *Rock* and a sureness of spirit in the plays significant of an arrival. The reconciliation is nevertheless the most significant aspect of his final poetry.

The sustaining of moments in the individual, we are told in that final poetry, is through the "drawing of this Love and the voice of this Calling" which has sounded in Eliot's ears long before *Little Gidding*, though it seemed early a calling of mermaids or sirens. That Calling, whose final reference lies in Christian orthodoxy, sustains one in the journey.

> We shall not cease from exploration
> And the end of all our exploring
> Will be to arrive where we started
> And know the place for the first time.

But this is an assurance in Eliot late in his career, the assurance that all manner of thing shall be well, and what we want to do now is see his own search, a search which led Eliot to assume the role of a Moses to the romantics. It is a search which springs from the moral consciousness of a dramatic mind. Now Eliot is very English about this moral consciousness. That is, asceticism must relate to beef puddings. Art isn't itself Paradise. Venice suspended in the imagination is not a final resting place for the soul. Poetry isn't one thing, life another. One notices such an objection to Valéry, expressed in Eliot's introduction to a volume of Valéry's prose. For life to Eliot is spiritual life. It is the integration of being whereby one is accommodated to the world, but not held by it. The history of Eliot's poetry is the history of his personal pursuit of that accommodation. And it started with the uneasiness of mind that required for its expression an unusual mode. As it developed, it resulted in his transcending William James's psychology and in his translating F. H. Bradley's epistemology to spiritual relevance.

III

❀ I turn now to Eliot's pursuit of a mode of expression. It is a mode which, despite the prominence of French literature in his imagination, has an initial clue in Browning, as we have said. But why was Eliot so dissatisfied with Browning? Unlike Browning's use of specific, named masks, Eliot tends to enact a pursuit through a vaguer mask, which after some puzzlement we identify by the name of Gerontion or Tiresias. On closer examination, the poem's mask is less far removed from the poet than it at first seems to be. Eliot's poems tend to involve stages of a pursuit, each more complex in its manner and implication than the one before it: from his portraits of Prufrock and Sweeney, to "Gerontion," to "The Hollow Men," to *The Waste Land,* to *Ash Wednesday,* to *The Four Quartets.* Through these stages, Eliot enacts his pursuit, as Browning does not. One might suppose that Browning is the more dramatic, Eliot the more lyrical. (I am of course considering the Browning of the monologues and long narratives.) In a sense this is so; Browning's poems do carry the names of ancient artists and bishops, and he attempts their voices. The poet does seem to be separate from, detached, as one expects the dramatic poet to be. But then one notices that the result of Browning's detachment is that he produces what seems to be a typical representative of an age or an ironic perspective upon a situation, out of the materials of history: a monk or bishop or frustrated painter, or a deranged lover on love's immortality or the strange case of Lazarus. More than wax figure or ironic state-ment—but not a great deal more. That is, Browning falls far short of tragic characters or dramatic irony such as one finds in Shake-speare, while at the same time he maintains an aloofness which has less to do with the requirements of drama than with a protection of the self. Some of Pound's irritation with Browning, as in the opening lines of Canto II, is on these grounds.

I say "out of the materials of history." The Browning poem tends to be an essay upon some aspect of psychology of the mind of a particular historical period revisited, or a situation brought about in a particular period by its institutions. Browning's is not an attempt at the timelessness of the human mind and spirit such as Eliot praises in Shakespeare when he says "Shakespeare acquired more essential history from Plutarch than most men could from the whole British Museum." There is something of the British Museum that lingers about the poetry of Browning. E. A. Robinson, himself a descendant of Browning, defines this characteristic of Shakespeare's talent when he has Ben Jonson say, with puzzlement, pride, and self-despair, that Shakespeare

> out of his
> Miraculous inviolable increase
> Fills Ilion, Rome, or any town you like
> Of olden time with timeless Englishmen.

Robinson is closer to his Ben Jonson than to his Shakespeare, closer to Browning than to Eliot, in his capacity for risking himself in his poetry. It is not his unwillingness to risk the self that is missing in Robinson, for he comes close to destroying himself in order to enter into those terrible grounds where illusion and vision confound the lesser spirits among the poets. We recall for comparison Keats's engagement of illusion in an attempt to escape illusion, and the inevitable failures. The attempt and the subsequent failure give to his great poems a dramatically spontaneous quality that we praise as immediacy, whereupon we examine Keats's art. But his art doesn't fully account for the force of his poetry. When Keats writes about "negative capability," about his ability to stand with Achilles in the trenches, he isn't talking about devices of art or techniques of writing poetry: he is talking about his attempt to

51

live. The despair in Keats's poetry has as its immediate cause a very real failure in John Keats the man to accept the limits of earthly life that were all too painfully borne in upon him. It is against such painful dangers to one's poetry from such intense engagements with life that Eliot attempts to guard himself in his early years. The most famous of his arguments concerning the dangers of the personal to the poet is his "Tradition and the Individual Talent," in which he insists on the necessity of separating the mind that composes from the man who is emotionally involved with life to the point that any composition he attempts is threatened aesthetically. The essay is in large part Eliot's attempt to establish "negative capability" as an aesthetic concern, but his attempt to neutralize the personal in his argument is far less successful in the essay than his accomplishment of that removal in *Prufrock and Other Observations*. The painful spiritual circumstances of this period in Eliot's life are comparable to Keats's bodily decay: they cannot be ignored in understanding the accomplishment of Eliot as critic and poet. Eliot found himself bound to his Fanny Brawne by bonds which were an intricate part of his complex commitment to tradition. The unhappy circumstances of Eliot's first marriage required him to examine the threats of such traditional institutions to the individual talent. His struggle was to distinguish between the personal and the private, a distinction he did not satisfactorily make in his argument. For one must distinguish between the essential involvement in life one finds himself sharing with mankind by virtue of common humanity and the accidents of that involvement such as the particulars of private relationships. As yet, Eliot could not establish for himself the proper relationship between the poet's life and the poet's art. It leads him to be concerned with answering questions such as Thomas Hardy had been asking in his poetry and fiction about the relation of the individual to his tradition: it leads him to confronting and opposing such answers as D. H. Lawrence gives to these questions through his notorious display of private relationships in defiance of traditionalism.

52

Another of the poets writing in English from whom Eliot perhaps learned something of the dangers of the "uncertain affairs of men" upon the orderliness of their art was E. A. Robinson. Robinson's private circumstances, the particulars of family problems, were much closer to Eliot's own than to Keats's. Robinson, no less than Keats, was plagued by the curse of uncertainty. But unlike Keats, he turns from grief for the self to record the grief in others. One sees it in the point of view of many of his poems. "James Wetheral," "Miniver Cheevy," "Mr. Flood," "Richard Cory" are characters seen from the outside, with the poet as an intermediary voice between his subject and his audience, saying in the words of a fiction writer not unlike Robinson, "Lost, lost, and by the wind grieved." He insists as well to the audience that it suspend conclusion and, consequently, judgment of his characters. For who can say with certainty whose is the illusion in the poem "Richard Cory"? Cory's final solution may as easily result from a final illusion no more real than his townsmen's illusion of his well-being. Robinson was intent on certainty, but plagued by a belief that the only certainty is the likelihood of illusion. And in consequence, his is the poetry of pathos.

Robinson's view of human existence and of the possibilities of knowing determine the mode of his poetry. In the interest of recording the grief of others, while leaving the causes of the grief ambiguous (thereby recording the brotherhood of misery), he turned to the dramatic possibilities of presenting that conflict between illusion and vision through personae, rather than choosing the personal voice which Keats uses in his engagement with failure. Thomas Hardy appealed to Robinson strongly. But the likelihood of Hap or Chance as god of the universe calls forth no such acid irony in Robinson as it does in Hardy. Not that Robinson removes himself in order to escape Hardy's irony, nor as Browning does in the interest of dramatic voice; for Robinson is present as mediator of grief. Choosing to be so present, he is handicapped, as Conrad felt himself handicapped in fiction; Robinson lacks the new techniques of fiction that Hawthorne and Conrad predict and Joyce initiates in prose, Eliot and Pound in poetry.° Robinson wishes to take us to the heart of his character and to that character's inner mind, believing at the same time that we can never arrive there. He does not assume the sufficiency of biographical knowledge of his personae, as Browning does in "The Bishop Orders His Tomb." The result? He either engages upon speculation in verse, as in "Exit," and in a better poem, "Eros Tyrannos." Or he dramatizes the character's own speculation, as in "Vickery's Mountain" and "Luke Havergal." In the speculative poems, the effect is reminiscent of Henry James's late attempts to weigh idea or character upon the scale of sentence, where grammatical modification often shows up as device. It sometimes appears that Robinson is trying by trial and error to bracket the reality, expecting never to hit it directly.

When he chooses to present "Luke Havergal" he is bolder in his technique, and also closer to Browning. For in that poem one has a voice speaking to Luke Havergal, it appears, but speaking words that one may suppose to be Luke Havergal's thoughts. The ambiguity is dramatically forceful in that we have, as in Eliot, a disembodied consciousness. But unlike Eliot, we have both the consciousness and the objective staging. The exchange of the voice with Luke is otherwise quite like the exchange of Eliot's "I" with his "You" in the "Love Song of J. Alfred Prufrock," though Eliot's journey to the tea party is less cliché-haunted than Robinson's journey to "the Western gate."

Eliot, however else he may differ from Shakespeare, is like that poet in his attempt at dramatic immediacy in which the poet is hidden. He has advantages over Robinson in many respects, but he has as well a boldness which is in addition to his advantage

° Hawthorne, at Salem, reflects on the possibility of a story: "To write a dream which shall resemble the real course of a dream, with all its inconsistency, its strange transformations . . . with nevertheless a leading idea running through the whole. Up to this old age of the world, no such thing has ever been written." And Conrad, in an early letter, predicts "a form for which we are not ripe as yet."

of knowledge of the new sciences of the mind or the new techniques the French poets were about. So he plunges into the murky depths of Prufrock, as Robinson cannot into Luke Havergal. That boldness is in part possible because initially, unlike Robinson, he does accept as the final truth of knowing that all certainty is impossible in the conflict between illusion and vision, and in this Eliot is again like Shakespeare. Eliot is concerned with a timelessness that may be achieved by absorbing time. Which is to say he is concerned with an accommodation of the spirit to its temporal limitations, a concern at least as old as Aeschylus. It is this aspect of Shakespeare that makes him a religious writer. Not a Catholic or Protestant or Atheist, all of which are religious positions—those denominations are too limiting for the concern I have to present. The religious impulse I mean is toward digesting the possible. Toward encompassing the *said* and *done* of history. The result is, for Shakespeare, a Macbeth, a Lear, a Prospero. What is the result for Eliot?

IV

❀ Eliot starts with the present time in his explorations, not only with his private circumstances in an age which is seemingly impoverished in its letters and a pragmatic desert in its thought. First of all he is concerned with the workings of his own mind relative to knowledge. The problems of epistemology are a challenge to him, as they were an insurmountable obstacle to his kinsman Wordsworth. Eliot is interested in the new arguments of psychology and philosophy, and we remember that he pursues his interest to the point of completing his dissertation on the English philosopher already alluded to, F. H. Bradley, the study being published under the title *Knowledge and Experience in the Philosophy of F. H. Bradley* (1964). But the end of this study is that he might write poetry. It is as if he prepares himself to carry out Wordsworth's prediction that the poet of the future would "be ready to follow the steps of the man of science . . . carrying sensation into the midst of the objects of science itself." Given such training, given the dramatic inclination that is in him that so inclined him to sympathy with "the later Elizabethan drama," and given the nature of his own age, Eliot sought a method whereby he could create *unstaged drama*.

The romantic's usual dream is of writing drama equal to Sophocles, and usually he sets himself to drama before he has learned enough about his art to recognize the dramatist's problem with voices, the subject Eliot considers in his lecture on the *Three Voices of Poetry*. Eliot is himself, from the beginning, the romantic spirit, for all his repeated suspicions of romanticism. By romantic spirit I mean at once a very broad and a very limited thing: I mean an inclination of a spirit which moves in a dissatisfaction caused by the absence of a desirable thing (as my colleague Calvin Brown has distinguished the romantic from the satiric). That absent desirable thing may be named specifically, as in a Miniver Cheevy's romanticism, or it may be undefined and so unnamable, as I take the case to be with the early Eliot. Eliot is at the same time dissatisfied by the undesirable presence of a decayed civilization, a condition which might lead a poet to become a Jeremiah or a Swift, depending upon his talent and temperament.

The writers we are more generally familiar with under that designation "romantic"—Carlyle, Keats, Wordsworth—seem inevitably concerned for that period of Western civilization that is late medieval or early Renaissance in making their particular points. That concern too is in Eliot. But there slowly emerges a difference in his concern. He isn't enamoured of a dream of the good old days so that one may actively restore them to the present, but is rather occupied with the particular dream held by the men of those supposedly good old days—a dream which enabled them to transcend their own undesirable world. He is concerned for the angle of their vision in terms of what their vision beheld, and his concern is as "scientific" in its nature as his intellect will allow. For Eliot knew, as many of those who suspect his concern for traditionalism do not, that those good old days were not spent by its heroes in Eden. He sought to understand the nature of the vision whereby the great minds he admired were able to accept the corrupt world and survive it. Dante survived the jungle of Florence. Though he wandered Italy, he was not sustained by the expectation of finding an ideal city. The first major romantic figure of our literature proclaimed long since that the mind is its own place, with powers to make a heaven of this world's hell; Lucifer thereby established himself in Apollo's stead for the nineteenth-century poet, whether one look to Wordsworth or Byron or Baudelaire.

But to Eliot's critical eye, Lucifer had played the poet false, even as he suspected that fallen angel of doing with his friends Pound and Joyce. Keats failed, Wordsworth failed; Byron's turns out to be, in Eliot's words, a "bogus diabolism," whose virtues are those of devil's advocate, an office whose existence is made possible only by the possibility of sainthood. The mind, Eliot began to see, is far more capable of making a hell than a heaven, an inevitable accomplishment when it is intent upon being its own place. During these early years of considering the nature of the poet's mind, which expressed itself to the world outside Eliot in such essays as "Tradition and the Individual Talent" and "Dante," Eliot was carrying about with him (as Conrad Aiken recalls for us) a copy of Dante's work. Now Eliot's essays of this period are careful in their avoidance of concerns for the spirit, emphasizing the problems of art or of knowing, but it is a concern for the spirit—of the mind's true relation to existence separate from the self—that is haunting Eliot, leading him toward that spiritual crisis that precedes *The Waste Land.* He is becoming engaged upon questions higher than those of epistemology.

Eventually Eliot comes to Dante's dream, feels at home with it. But it is a slow journey of the mind for him, requiring a profound adjustment of Bradleyan phenomenology to that inclusive event of Christ's crucifixion, through which man became eligible for a knowledge that subsumes the mind's powers of exercising itself— the science of psychology. It was not until after *Ash Wednesday* that the peace of God that passeth understanding revealed itself publicly in the heart and mind of Eliot. Meanwhile, we observe that Eliot's obsession with history, richly reflected in his poems and essays on those minds he admires—Aeschylus, Dante, the Elizabethan and Jacobean playwrights, Donne—isn't an interest in history itself but an intense concern for a vision which would afford an accommodating of the mind and then the spirit to history: a means of transcending the world more dependable than Wordsworth's *nature* or Keats's *urn.* "The Journey of the Magi" is a romantic journey recalled long after, without much understanding; hence a journey which is understated by its protagonist as being "(you may say) satisfactory." The poem, late in the canon of Eliot's poetry, reflects a state of mind which seems to me analogous to Eliot's own state of mind between the Prufrock volume and *The Waste Land*. Eliot is, in that period, only somewhat less passive than the magus who speaks in the poem. The old ways of poetry of his immediate predecessors are under attack by Eliot as his attempt at understanding a suspected inadequacy in them. Nevertheless they have taught him much. Keats is important in respect to his richness of detail; Wordsworth, in respect to his concerns with techniques of projecting emotions. Browning combines both, and adds a concern for the history of civilization. There is also in Browning an elementary delving into the mind as a repository of significant confusions of time present and time past. I mean this in respect to both the surface techniques of his poetry and the implications of those techniques to life. There is, for instance, the distortions of love in "Porphyria's Lover," in "The Soliloquy of the Spanish Cloister," in "My Last Duchess," in "The Bishop Orders His Tomb," and in other monologues that must have an inevitable concern to a mind already haunted by "the drawing of Love and the voice of this Calling" specified in *Little Gidding*. The man who was "struggling to attack" a point of view in aesthetics "related to the metaphysical theory of the substantial unity of the soul" ("Tradition and the Individual Talent") was nevertheless deeply concerned with the fragmentation of being which he thought the cause of such failures as the dissociation of sensibility.

Browning, too, was interested in such fragmentation, as his general focus upon the Renaissance as a foil to and indictment of nineteenth-century England suggests. In his poetry there is a distortion of voice, the speaking voice echoed as a reflector of confusion. And it is a distortion not so daringly attempted in poetry since the Elizabethan dramatists or their immediate successor who so fascinated Eliot, John Donne, who inherits poetic drama as it begins to move off the English stage toward the collected poems of Wordsworth, Shelley, and Browning.

The retreat of drama into the lyric—and drama's disappearance from the lyric itself, as poetry moves on to new modes in the essays of Pope and then to the confessional lyric of the nineteenth century—parallels the fracturing of that individual wholeness which so concerned Dante, as it had Aquinas before him, and before him Augustine. The decline is reflected in a timidity of the soul. The nadir of this disintegration, accelerated by nineteenth-century science and established in literature by the naturalists, coincides with Eliot's appearance upon the literary scene. With Wordsworth and Browning as hints to the possible methods of expressing his awareness, with his study of the problem of the relation of *Knowledge and Experience*, as affected by new theories that were to blossom as the science of psychology, with his own dissatisfied mind as goad, with his desire to be a dramatic poet rather than the philosopher he had trained to be, Eliot examines Beaumont, Webster, Shakespeare, Donne. At the same time that he is looking into the history of poetry, he turns to poetry, seeking answers to his personal spiritual questions that carry in their form the drama of his own personal seeking.

It is that spiritual timidity which Dante represents in Ante-Hell that concerns Eliot first and last—his own timidity and our age's. Illustrations are almost as extensive as his poems: there is Prufrock shadowed by Guido, John the Baptist, Hesiod. Sweeney shadowed by Theseus and Agamemnon. What we want to keep in mind is that we are dealing with the drama of Eliot's quest, a drama which is akin to, but in a mode quite different from, that of Wordsworth in his *Prelude* and *Excursion*. I make this point again since we do not generally deal adequately with the importance of the *personal* element in twentieth-century literature, Eliot and others having worked to make us forget it. Having been conditioned to eschew the personal heresy, we nevertheless tend to take such a poet as Eliot to have established his position initially, after which he merely elaborates it from first to last with an intellectual detachment constant in its intensity and steady in its basic assumptions.

60

But such an approach not only involves us in a kind of personal heresy we aren't aware of: the elements of the personal are in themselves false. The conscious disengagement of personality in critical essays such as "Tradition and the Individual Talent" is quite separate from the artful control of personality in the poems themselves. No doubt we are too quick to use critical reminiscence such as Eliot's as an instrument to the poems. We attempt to reconcile contradictions in the essays as if they were the deliberate gradual unfolding secret to an anciently held position, rather than the process of self-discovery one might inevitably descry in the body of a poet's lyric poetry. Particularly given such a position as Eliot has enjoyed as critic, we tend to respect contradiction as capable of reconciliation, depending too heavily upon the transcendence of contradiction by paradox, a favorite critical word since Eliot's appearance as essayist. (I have in mind as an example an essay by Allen Austin, "T. S. Eliot's Theory of Personal Expression," in *PMLA* for June 1966 which does not concern itself quite fiercely enough with Eliot's problem with the term *personality*.) For what Eliot tries to avoid in his dealings with the term is the true center of personality as it relates to poetry, its seeing—its vision. It is a strategy in Eliot, no doubt determined by the secular nature of our times, which nevertheless fails to prevent a Karl Shapiro from finding him out and accusing him of trying to put one over on the age, tricking it toward a religiosity Shapiro finds repugnant.

One turns to the critical treatment of Eliot's poetry and finds a parallel distortion. Given that Dante's vision must have been a whole one to write such a work as the *Comedy,* given Eliot's early interest in Dante, given the careful techniques of detachment in Eliot's poetry, one is inclined to try to make of the body of Eliot's poetry an unfolding of a unified vision already held when his first poems were written. If we have Eliot before us as enemy, as Karl Shapiro does, we may take the poetry to constitute a deliberate unity whose purpose is subversive. If, on the other hand, we admire Eliot, we tend to credit him with a wisdom he comes to as if he

61

possesses it from the beginning. Thus Harvey Gross, in a reading of "Gerontion" (*PMLA*, June 1958), wants us to apply the later Eliot too heavily to the poem, as if Eliot were already much closer to the hope of *The Waste Land*, the acceptance of *Ash Wednesday*, the revelation of the *Four Quartets*, and the steady assurance of *The Rock* than he actually is in 1920. Mr. Gross takes the final section of "Gerontion" to be spoken with hope, not despair, expressive of a realization of future possibility in the voice of the poem. But we must remember that *The Waste Land* comes a bit later, out of what Eliot's friends took to be a nervous breakdown. *The Waste Land* is a part of his recovery from that experience which involved Eliot in a dark night of the soul such as St. John of the Cross describes (in a work which has relevance to *Ash Wednesday*, particularly to Section III of that poem). Eliot's was not simply physical exhaustion from long hours in a London bank, as Pound seems to have considered it. Nor could Ernest Hemingway, concerned with confronting kudu and lions, understand the terrors of Christ the tiger, as his childish recollections of "Major Eliot" (in *A Moveable Feast*) indicate.

Pound's private foundation for Eliot, Belle Esprit, could not have helped Eliot quite so much as that third-hand psychoanalysis by the American Homer Lane. Aiken records it (*Sewanee Review*, Winter 1966): "Tell your friend Aiken [Lane told an intermediary, Dilston Radcliff] to tell *his* friend Eliot that all that's stopping him is his fear of putting anything down that is short of perfection. He thinks he's God." Aiken reports that Eliot was angered by the message, but that immediately he was able to write once again, composing *The Waste Land* following this third-hand analysis of his state. What Lane did, in effect, was point out to Eliot that Lucifer is wrong. While the mind may be its own place, it does not follow that it can, as we have said, make a Heaven of that place. Its powers are god-like, but not co-extensive with God's.

The problem of the personal has been an acute one in modern letters because the poet (and usually the fiction writer, we might add) has used his own life as the materials of art, while entertaining ambitions of an art larger than lyric. In an age of instant publicity the risks to art are greater, the mask more essential to protect the poem's integrity. But the mask itself can tempt the poet into pretending that the personal is merely materials of art, as if his own sanity or salvation were not engaged in the art he creates. The thing that I find remarkable about Eliot as a poet, as separate from Eliot the critic, is that he accepted poetry as being related to his life in a very personal way. Whatever pains he went to in order to guard himself from the reader were as much out of personal timidity and shyness as out of aesthetic concerns. Finally he is not above or beyond or outside his work, as Joyce's romantic Stephen would have the poet be, but he is quietly, unobtrusively, shyly present. His artistry, fortunately, is such that he controls his presence in his poetry as no English romantic dramatist since Shakespeare was able to do. I want now to talk about the art of this accomplishment.

V

In Browning's portrait of the Bishop of St. Praxed's or of the Duke of Ferrara or the inhabitant of the Spanish cloister, the boldness and complexity of the active spirits strike a reader at once. Subtleties of the spiritual or intellectual estate of the characters do of course exist, but the words they speak are so obviously allusions to their time and place, circumstance and ideas, that one has little difficulty getting at those subtleties. Footnotes to a Browning poem tend to be identification of allusion given indirectly in the poem, the indirection itself establishing a familiarity with the idea or object alluded to so as to give verisimilitude. It is Browning's way of making a voice convincing, as when a speaker refers to "a great text in Galatians" or speaks of frustrating the Arian or quotes the book of Job. Eliot, too, bears footnoting, and himself supplied quantities of notes in his essays no less than in the more spectacular appendage to *The Waste Land.* But since he is intent upon the inactive spirit and its problem of inertia as a necessary substitute for dramatic action, his allusions represent pressures and distortions which require identification more complex than simply an identification of their origins. Allusions in Eliot are more images reflecting the speaker's emotions than indications of the speaker's knowledge. The point I am making can be seen, perhaps, by a comparison of Browning's

> Swift as a weaver's shuttle fleet our years:
> Man goeth to the grave, and where is he?

to Prufrock's

> I have seen my head (grown slightly bald) brought
>   in upon a platter
> And here is no great matter.

One hasn't gone very far into the effectiveness of Prufrock's line by noting John the Baptist as allusion, though the Bishop's lines are pretty well exhausted by pointing to Job. It is necessary for the reader of "Prufrock" to consider the mock heroic overtones and the question of the extent of Prufrock's self-irony.

As if commenting on this distinction in his own allusions as compared to Browning's Eliot has his speaker say in "Gerontion"

> Vacant shuttles
> Weave the wind. . . .

There is an intense fusion of allusion and character in the lines that Browning does not manage. To give art's illusion of a dis-ordered and dying mind, Eliot has drawn on Job also. He adds to those verses Browning borrowed (Job 7:6 and 14:10) an allusion to Job 7:7—"O remember that my life is wind: mine eyes shall no more see good." He has incorporated these passages in the large metaphor of his poem: body and soul as house and inhabitant. He thereby relates the inevitable winds of the world's destruction, the winds of time, to the emptiness of Gerontion's windy head. Thoughts are the shuttles, vacant because there is no thread of meaning weaving a pattern which the speaking voice can recognize itself in relation to.° Naked, Gerontion—Eliot's Job—lacerates himself upon his peculiar ant hill, the awareness of his own vacuity. His is a "peevish gutter" from which waste words emit. (Compare Eliot's bold figure in *Ash Wednesday* (III): the stair is "dark / Damp, jagged, like an old man's mouth drivelling, beyond repair. . . .") The shuttles, dry thoughts, resist any loading under the controls of history or religion or the names of Silvero, Hakagawa, Madame de Tornquist, Fräulein von Kulp. Finally, Gerontion has failed to commit any great sin, except denial, but even those denials have

---

° Donald Davidson has pointed out to me an alternate translation of Job 7:6. Rabbi Victor E. Reichart says, in a commentary on Job (*Soncino Edition* of Job. Hindhead, Surrey, 1947, p. 30): "*Tikwah* means 'cord' as well as 'hope,' and an alternative translation proposed is 'they come to an end through want of a thread.'"

been minor. Judas can commit an act suitable to his punishment in Dante's Hell because he is aware that it is Christ he betrays. But surely Gerontion comes to see that his betrayal lacks that large arrogance. He has drifted away from an early passion, in the interest of what Shakespeare in a similar controlling metaphor called a "costly mansion," now rapidly decaying about the vague identity called Gerontion. It is no longer to be denied that his is a rented house. What may the ghost—the spirit—expect then, if there be a ghost? Gerontion thinks no mercy due him, none possible. Such a spiritual state as Gerontion's, which Eliot took to be common among us, does not suit one's ghost for Hell or Purgatory. This was, in fact, Eliot's objection to Pound's hell in the early *Cantos*. One cannot treat a Prufrock or a Gerontion as if he were as remarkable a figure as Browning's Bishop. And Pound's waxing wroth over such spiritual insignificances, peopling his lowest Hell with them, was to dignify such creatures beyond their merit by the condemnation itself. For such characters, as Eliot describes them in his next poem after "Gerontion," are to be remembered

> not as lost
> Violent souls, but only
> As the hollow men. . . .

Given such an age as Eliot takes ours to be, and his necessity of making it serve as material for his art, the pressures upon the possibility of making the present state of man significantly dramatic, of raising it beyond a Robinson's pathos, are formidable indeed. Particularly are they formidable when we add to them Eliot's inclination to generalize—his struggle to particularize a view of social and spiritual conditions in the twentieth century. For only by ignoring Eliot's true center and concentrating only upon his poetics is it possible to deny the very strong didactic bent which his art must control.

Eliot requires of the modern ear that it be finely attuned—more finely attuned than was required of Browning's immediate audience. Few among his own immediate audience heard, as did Eliot, the faint cry of spirit beginning to grow out of self-consciousness just before World War I, though there were indeed signs in the literature of naturalism—the despair of a Dreiser and the fervor of a D. H. Lawrence. Eliot's affinities, however, are not here, but in the subtle explorations of James and Conrad. He requires of his reader, as do these writers, that he attempt to inhabit the timid mind's world, a world the self is constantly tempted into making safe from actions or loud words. Lord Jim and Axel Heyst are spiritual kinsmen of Prufrock and Gerontion. Eliot's admiration of James, which he talks about in respect to style, has its deeper cause in James's awareness of the modern spiritual estate and its limitations upon art.

VI

✿ Perhaps at this point we should consider in more detail certain aspects of "Prufrock" and "Gerontion," in relation to a general problem of subjectivity in the personae of the poems and the complex literary vehicle which results, the schizophrenic monologue. Certainly the problem of point of view in Eliot's poetry has been a knotty one. There continue to be attempts made to find some acceptable reading of the *I* and the *you* as it relates to the *we* in Prufrock's final words; so too the problem of the identity of the person addressed by Gerontion and the relation of that address to the *we* involved in the poem seems not finally settled.

First, let us consider those final three lines of "Prufrock":

> We have lingered in the chambers of the sea
> By sea-girls wreathed with seaweed red and brown
> Till human voices wake us, and we drown.

I take these final lines to be an epitaph by the *I* upon itself. They reflect a subcelestial existence in which the *I* moves, whose corollary is that of the crab on the ocean floor. The lines recall all the long scuttlings under air and fog, of which a particular instance is implied in the movement of the poem. The "chambers of the sea" is an ironic naming of those rooms Prufrock knows of old, where "the women come and go," their words and gowns as entangling as seaweed. The lingering has been emotionally presented throughout the poem, from the delaying fog images through coffee spoons, dooryards, teacups. And the "sea-girls" are "girls" only as Prufrock is young: that is, the word is ironic. Seaweed—the false reds and browns that on one level may be shawls and morning-coats—hiding the body's mortality. And on another level, seaweed is conversation about the ultimate realities, reduced in Prufrock's too-comfortable aquarium to "some talk of you and me," thereby avoiding the spirit's dying agony.

For we notice how shocked the speaker is to discover light brown hair on a woman's arm when the shawl is cast aside, and we see him projecting, anticipating, an unbearable indifference to a more shocking revelation of spirit, if he should turn Lazarus. (The Lazarus passage recalls not only the New Testament account of Lazarus, but that ambitious treatment of the event in Browning's "An Epistle Containing the Strange Medical Experience of Karshish, the Arab Physician.") Whenever light, whether lamplight or a brief aperture for the spirit, occurs in the poem, Prufrock is disordered, more anxious to submerge than Dante's Guido. Prufrock wills to lose all identity, to sacrifice all self as the only self-protection.

In his world we are in the regions of Shelley's "oozy woods which wear a sapless foliage," and Prufrock wants it kept that way. But Eliot allows us to see those depths, not from the surface as in Shelley's romantic coloring, nor from any vantage point of height such as Dante enjoys as he looks down upon the diviners (among whom is Tiresias) in the *Inferno*. In Prufrock's elected chambers, the seaweed weights consciousness—twisting, coiling, encircling. *Wreathed* is a word with complicated ancestry, carrying undertones of a cousin descendent, *writhe*. Those undertones are supported by the entangling music of Eliot's line: "sea-girls wreathed with seaweed." And how safe such strangulation to a Prufrock—when the shawl covers the light brown hair, when the talk undulates with "you and me." Those enigmatic *"human* voices" imply, I think, the humanistic burden assumed as the proper cultured stance of the intellectual in the first quarter of this century. Eliot later examines the humanism of Irving Babbitt, we recall, finding it "alarmingly like very liberal Protestant theology of the nineteenth century: it is, in fact, a product—a by-product—of Protestant theology in its last agonies." Humanism is no acceptable "alternative to religion." It represents a compromise between those two extremes which Matthew Arnold celebrated as "ignorant armies": new science divorced of history and old religion bankrupt in its theology. To Eliot, then, humanism was a new bent to culture which prevented any possible significance to either mermaids or to a Lazarus. In witness whereof, Prufrock can neither broach Lazarus as of serious concern or say to his dark lady of this love song, "Teach me to hear mermaids singing."

Surely the poet who championed the intricacies of Donne and Joyce would expect us to search such words as *human* and *wreathed* with care. It is even conceivable, in the light of Joyce's enlargement and refinement of the technique of "Prufrock" in his "Work in Progress," that Eliot may himself mean a very daring complexity to such a word as *wake* in the final line, as it relates both to the *drown* and to Prufrock's general uneasiness throughout the poem over what may be said of him when he is no longer present. Certainly, had Prufrock any real strength—any ghost in him—he could cry out on the beach with Wordsworth "I'd rather be a pagan," and so risk hearing those mermaids. But "Prufrock" is a death poem. Its central consciousness has strength sufficient only to recognize a failure and to execute one final treachery, attempting a final escape into the *we*. It is a suicide of the *I*. For to inhabit the vapid world of the teaparty is not finally to revert to a primordial awareness which truly corresponds to the crab's. The epitaph of the last three lines embodies a final self-betrayal. The dramatic irony lies in our knowing it a self-betrayal under way in the poem from the beginning.

If we turn now from "Prufrock" to "Gerontion," we notice a decided shift away from strict privacy such as that indicated by the epigraph that initiates "Prufrock." There is also a general tone of self-judgment in "Gerontion" such as one does not find in "Prufrock," though the judgment which the narrator of "Gerontion" turns upon himself does not necessarily mean he fully understands

70

his spiritual state. There is, however, the distinction of an intellectual analysis under way in the poem, as opposed to Prufrock's simpler emotional responses. I say this once more, lest we be tempted to ascribe to Eliot himself a position of acceptance in advance of what his own position actually was. Let us on this point recall some of Eliot's own words, written much later than "Gerontion," from "Second Thoughts on Humanism" (1929):

> Most people suppose that some people, because they enjoy the luxury of Christian sentiments and the excitement of Christian ritual, swallow or pretend to swallow incredible dogma. For some the process is exactly opposite. Rational assent may arrive late, intellectual conviction may come slowly, but they come inevitably without violence to honesty and nature. To put the sentiments in order is a later and an immensely difficult task: intellectual freedom is earlier and easier than complete spiritual freedom.

It seems to me that the development of Eliot's poetics and his spiritual point of view are reasonably summarized by this statement. For instance, one has in his poetry an increasingly closer correspondence between the mask of the poem and the poet himself as he moves toward that "complete spiritual freedom" of the *Quartets*. Another way of saying this is that he reaches an intellectual acceptance of Him "whose service is perfect freedom," as the Anglican Prayer Book puts it. The point is relevant here, since it is one we must necessarily engage in considering the point of view in "Gerontion," in trying to discover who is addressed by the consciousness of that poem.

John Crowe Ransom's recent essay on "Gerontion" (*Sewanee Review*, Spring 1966) is, as one knows to expect, a very suggestive reading, the kind of reading that opens up anew such questions as may have been too easily closed. While his essay is primarily a metrical analysis of the poem, under a general metaphor of its structure as symphony, speculations along the way concerning themes or intention set one's mind to turning. He suggests, for instance, that the person addressed in the imperative "Think now" is Christ Himself and develops that point. But such a reading leaves the problem of the poem's *we* suspended in that later passage which also includes the imperative address:

> Think at last
> We have not reached conclusion, when I
> Stiffen in a rented house.

It seems to me that the voice of the poem is carrying on a colloquy much like that one in "Prufrock," but with a difference which lies in Gerontion's willing acceptance of failure, as opposed to Prufrock's insidious arguments against responsibility. (For reasons that will presently appear, let us bear in mind that Orestes manages an acceptance such as Gerontion's in the *Eumenides*, and so allows for the stilling of the Furies and an end to the curse upon the House of Atreus; similarly, Dante performs a ritual of acceptance on the banks of Lethe, under the stern eye of Beatrice.) An additional difference between Gerontion and Prufrock is that Gerontion's failures, which have wasted his ghost too, leave his final awareness centered upon the body and its false things of the world, whereas Prufrock's awareness tends toward timid flirtations with things of the spirit. One might perhaps make a profitable entry into "Gerontion" by considering the speaker of that poem related to the *you* of Prufrock's poem. But as we do so, let us consider that both the *you* of "Prufrock" and the *I* of "Gerontion" are more closely related to a failing light of the intellect, whose health both Dante and Eliot find necessary, though not finally sufficient to salvation. Surely neither Prufrock's *you* nor Gerontion's *I* is to be associated with Sweeney, though the sympathies of each when perverted lead toward the worldly estate of a Sweeney. Indeed, what I am suggesting is that Gerontion's attention is now focused on the inescapable but surmountable Sweeney which each man finds himself burdened by. At least, let us move in that direction in this consideration.

There seems to me a sufficiently sardonic note struck in those opening lines of "Gerontion" to justify an approach from this direction. The poem is one in which that faint consciousness, so tentatively resident, forces itself to accept its current spiritual condition, an impoverished one, the result of "a thousand small deliberations" such as Prufrock is so adept at. In matters spiritual, the speaker in "Gerontion" is the prodigal son turned contrite in his bankruptcy. In contrast to him, consider how Browning's Bishop (no mean prodigal himself) sneers in a moment of triumph over Gandolf:

> Aha, *elucescebat* quoth our friend?

But Gerontion's contraction of *juvenescence* to *juvescence* (which Mr. Ransom calls attention to in connection with the line's meter) is neither the vulgarity of a Gandolf nor the petty arrogance of the Bishop. It reflects Gerontion's awareness of his own corruption as he measures himself against more violent men. He believes not only that he has lost the possibility of Heaven but also the possibility of Hell. That is, he has lost the possibility of becoming child-like. The title itself reduces him through its diminutive form from "old man" to a *"little* old man." And he, somewhat like Virgil in Dante's poem, lives with knowledge but without hope.

Let us now once more recall another great mind so attractive to Eliot. Aeschylus, though not at the "hot gates," was at the salt marshes of Marathon as warrior. Having survived that encounter with the dangers of the East, he went on to write a play which puts words very like Gerontion's conspicuously in the mouths of little old men. Aeschylus' chorus to the *Agamemnon* describes itself as like children, ignorant of the world, walking a dream at mid-day, incapable of participation in sacrifice. It is hardly an exaggeration to say that twentieth-century literature chooses to cast Aeschylus' chorus as protagonist of its drama. And similarly, the concern for the sensual, a secondary theme with Aeschylus as in the private relationships of Agamemnon-Cassandra or Clytemnestra-Aegistheus, has become the main burden of interest in a world

73

increasingly obsessed by Marxian and Freudian dogmas since the decay of orthodox Christianity. In this respect, Eliot's House of Gerontion enlarges to include Western civilization, as Aeschylus' House of Atreus enlarges to include mid-fifth century Athenian civilization; its voice is one attempting to express the collective, troubled unconscious awareness of decay, as Aeschylus' play attempted to express the disturbed awareness of the loss of order and point toward its restoration through the *Eumenides*.

So then Gerontion tells over the sad account of his wasted spirit, with an honesty that is at least admirable. But, with the senses cooled, it appears undeniable to him that his desire was toward no high possibility. Aeschylus' chorus insists that sorrow, "memory's pain" (to which compare Gerontion's "reconsidered passion"), collects in the heart so that "though against our very will, even in our own despite," wisdom comes, by the "awful grace of God." In a similar vein, Gerontion affirms that "Virtues/ Are forced upon us by our impudent crimes." But the distance between Agamemnon's arrogance and Gerontion's impudence is great indeed, being finally the distance between the possibility of tragedy and mere pathos in the literary realm and between Hell (or Purgatory) and Ante-Hell in the theological realm. In the light of his vision of fate, Gerontion accepts history's (or, in Mr. Ransom's naming, Lachesis') meager gifts, she having given as he concludes "with such supple confusions / That the giving famishes the craving." (This may be Eliot's inversion of Dante's she-wolf which "When crammed . . . craves more fiercely than before.") Gerontion considers himself consumed with that which he was nourished by. The irony, as he sees it, is that he possesses a meager wisdom earned by his minor suffering, but possesses it only at a point in time where it cannot benefit him. It is too late to profit from the old advice to let the body waste in the spirit's growth. We, however, may remember from Dante's *Comedy* (and from other influences on Eliot: Augustine's *Confessions*, St. John's *Dark Night of the Soul*) that Gerontion's is a necessary preliminary to consequential existence. All fall short of St. Paul's mark, but how like Hell itself to recognize as an unworthy mark the worldly one Gerontion has so willingly fallen short of.

What is now lost to Gerontion is all pleasure of the worldly, those pleasures presented with such terror to Hawthorne's Young Goodman Brown in a dark woodland orgy. For through physical destruction by his own excess and inexorable time, Gerontion has lost his "sight, smell, hearing, taste and touch." In avoiding Goodman Brown's disillusion, Gerontion turned from innocent hope to pursue significance in the dark forces of the blood. The Fate attendant upon those dark forces has, since Hawthorne's beginnings and James's careful concerns, found high priests in Sir James Frazer and Sigmund Freud, whom Eliot transforms as he uses. Remembering Eliot's suspicions about humanism (handmaid to pragmatism), we might remember also that it was Puritanism, through its intense concern for burning away the worldly, which ironically established the pragmatic as that national way of life which James observed reaching into international life. Eliot is, as Matthiessen observed, in a line of descent through James from Hawthorne. Some of those poems in *Prufrock and Other Observations* are New England portraits implying questions such as those that plagued Hawthorne. For instance, as we may observe from "Prufrock" through *Ash Wednesday,* sexuality is as uneasy a theme to Eliot as it is to Hawthorne. The attempt to reach a conciliation of Iphigenia's blood at Aulis, in Freudian terms, has reduced the heroic situation from the tragic to the pathetic, as Gerontion knows too late (and as Eugene O'Neill demonstrates in his New England version of Aeschylus). "The Boston Evening Transcript," "Aunt Helen," and "Cousin Nancy" are surely in their implications markers along that road Eliot follows as he works his way from Hawthorne's New England dilemmas. "Gerontion" is a major marker, indicating Eliot's movement beyond the redaction of spirit by Frazer and Freud.

Which brings me once more back to those opening, sardonic

lines—to the goat coughing in the field overhead. Gerontion hears, though now reduced in his sensual awareness to the point where the sensation dimly perceived no longer carries to the imagination a suggestion of numinous, whether of the presence of Apollo or Dionysus. Inevitably in such circumstances, such a one as Gerontion falls back on art, on literary forms, man's attempt to make experience numinous. Gerontion, for instance, makes ironic use of the ancient literary analogy of soul-body, house-occupant, as we have noticed. His problem is that he can discover no vital presence in the sinful shell of his body, the part of his existence which may be named Sweeney Supine.

In his essay, Mr. Ransom calls attention to "Prufrock" and his struggle before dealing with "Gerontion." The woman whom Prufrock has particularly in mind, Mr. Ransom says, is not likely to receive his advances because of a question that lies between them, unanswered because unasked. "How does she feel about religion? If he asked it, and she was displeased with him for asking it, he would be displeased with her for not answering it, and they could reject each other simultaneously." What a suggestive way of speaking of Prufrock's dark lady. For, if Prufrock is no Hamlet, far less is he such a lover as that one who speaks honestly upon the attractions of the sensual with the voice of one accepting the bald spot in the middle of his hair:

> When my love swears that she is made of truth,
> I do believe her, though I know she lies,
> That she might think me some untutoured youth,
> Unlearned in the world's false subtleties.

Not only is a "Prufrock" saved from other-worldly questions but from worldly ones, involving the sensual, as well. If the poem's *you* may be presumed capable of such witty boldness as Shakespeare's lover and of recognizing the world's false subtleties in the *I* that speaks the poem (as I presume since I take the parenthetic interjections of that poem to represent the *you*'s breaking in), what of such a *you* when it reaches that time of life which is "as the glowing of such fire / That on the ashes of his youth doth lie"? In that latter state, he is beyond the lusts of the senses, beyond anything worldly except "reconsidered passion." And thus it is that Gerontion tells over his sad account, the gist of which is that he has spent too much spirit painting those outer walls so costly gay. Those walls too have been "blistered . . . patched and peeled." And Gerontion's Jew that squats on the window sill is the Mephisto our age has tried to deny, now come back to take possession of what Gerontion has bargained away. But possession of what?

In that question lies the cause of the sardonic quality of the poem. Bargains struck with Mephisto in the interest of the senses involve a forfeit of the soul. But the age which has taken Satan not to exist (His Satanic Majesty's most clever ruse, Baudelaire says), has taken the soul not to exist either. It is something of a shock to discover, then, that

> We have not reached conclusion, when I
> Stiffen in a rented house.

Gerontion says late in the poem, almost hopefully, "I have no ghosts." *Ghosts* is spoken in a context and with allusions that carry overtones of *soul.* Compare Job 14:10: "Man giveth up the ghost, and where is he?" And relate that verse to Browning's borrowings from Job, spoken by his Bishop:

> Swift as a weaver's shuttle fleet our years:
> Man goeth to the grave, and where is he?

Gerontion's words, which we have already looked at in respect to Eliot's technique, are

> Vacant shuttles
> Weave the wind. I have no ghosts. . . .

So once more we conclude that the place of "Gerontion," as

77

of all Eliot's poems through the *Waste Land*, is that geographical region of the *Divine Comedy* called Ante-Hell. Gerontion's first words have shown that true; no ghost of value inhabits his almost empty house. In the logical structure of those first sixteen lines, as opposed to their metrical·structure (to borrow Mr. Ransom's approach to Shakespeare's sonnets once more), the lines are indeed an Elizabethan sonnet. The summary "couplet" says,

> I am an old man
> A dull head among windy spaces.

The lines preceding are an inclusive accounting in which the speaker sees himself, not as such a great ruined cathedral as the Bishop of St. Praxed's might be likened to, but at best a gargoyle-decorated drain spout. The rain of grace, hot though it might be, would fill those windy spaces with a terror more rewarding than the winds of the world: Hell is better than Ante-Hell. But as it stands, Gerontion is being read to by his Orestes, being fed by an indifferent Clytemnestra. For it would indeed seem that his Clytemnestra has given up the knife for the soup spoon, poking the "peevish gutter" with a bland unconcern for those sounds of empty existence we listen to. The little old man here is, in his view of himself, at best an alimentary canal with a weak voice box, decayed even beyond the possibility of exciting that last membrane of the senses, reduced to an attempt to "protract" its profit with "pungent sauces." Now all that remains of life is the non-angelic worm of the alimentary system, whose futile wish is for Hell's fiery cathartic. The goat coughing in the field is at best only a goat, scarcely Dionysiac. And the things of nature and the refuse of this house are objects which can't even be surely certified as objects—"rocks, moss, stonecrop, iron, merds," unmodified by the senses.

Somehow, others (and among them an Agamemnon) have awakened tragedy out of such. But in Gerontion there has never been any hymn to existence which was capable of enlarging to *tragedy*. No hope then, it being too late to profit from its meager wisdom, meager since gained by no high suffering. But though there seems no ghost capable of a sustenance toward rejuvenation (and of what use now such long-ignored metaphor as "Within be fed, without be rich no more"), we ourselves may suspect a possibility, remembering that complete destruction of Dante under Beatrice's eyes on the shore of Lethe. If there is any hope for Gerontion, it is such as we may be aware of, not he, since we are above the possibility of his awareness (a difference in perspective which I have argued elsewhere as distinguishing the literature of pathos from tragedy: "In Pursuit of Melpomene"). We are capable of reflecting upon his state of being through the hints the poem gives us of Dante's vision: the "concitation of the backward devils"; the constant presence in the poem of the *Inferno's* darkness. And those words from Middleton's *Changeling*, "I that was near your heart was removed therefrom," seem a reduced echo of Beatrice's rebuke to Dante in the *Purgatorio*, delivered to the pleading Angel chorus:

> . . . when I'd reached my second age, and there,
> E'en on the threshold, life for life exchanged,
> Then he forsook me and made friends elsewhere.

Gerontion's final self-prophecy, "Gull against the wind, in the windy straits," though located by *Belle Isle*, point away from, rather than toward, Purgatory Mountain, and the possibility of such destruction as Dante's Ulysses encountered in gaining Hell. Ineligible, by his own honest estimate, for the dignity of Hell proper, the speaker waits the foreclosure of a trade now proved of little significance.

In the manner of an Elizabethan epilogue, Gerontion speaks in that key paragraph, the climax of the poem, beginning "The tiger springs in the new year." Gerontion considering himself of the worst, it is a part of the poem one might almost describe as full of passionate intensity. But it seems to me that its intensity is not out of what Yeats considered an energetic ignorance. Gerontion speaks directly to us as one who has failed, lest we fail too. He addresses us as members of his house, knowing that time devours us all:

> Think at last
> I have not made this show purposelessly
> And it is not by any concitation
> Of the backward devils.
> I would meet you upon this honestly.

This *show*, this dramatization of the decline of the West through soliloquy, is freely given us by Gerontion, where Prufrock has proved so niggardly as not even to acknowledge our presence. It is a sacrifice of admission, with the hope that it will be carried back into the world, a warning and not the agitation of self-pity such as that of the young man with backward vision, Claudio, to whom the words of Eliot's epigraph are spoken (*Measure for Measure*, III, i). Claudio loses his life, but he loses it by not pursuing that honor required for the spirit's health. From his after-dinner sleep, which is neither a sleep of youth nor age, Claudio is encouraged by the Duke to awaken and be "absolute for death" rather than continue asleep as "Merely . . . Death's fool." Gerontion would also reject self-pity as well as that backward vision such as Dante weeps for when he sees those poor devils, the diviners and fortune tellers (*Inferno*, XX). One notices in Eliot's passage a firmness of voice in Gerontion not unlike that in Duke Vincentio's speech from which the epigraph is taken, and very like that with which Virgil rebukes Dante whenever Dante's mind fails to see the significance of words or actions along the dark journey.

Gerontion, who was once near our heart, has been removed therefrom by nature's inexorable decay accelerated by wilful error. He exists now with all passion lost, not spent as Dante spends pity and terror toward a brightening mind. Gerontion supposes the sensual to be near our heart (as Virgil supposes the desire for true intellectual sight to be near Dante's). It was so with Gerontion of old as with us now; but now those false guides, the senses, cannot draw him closer to us. Meanwhile our own senses may remove us through wanton fears from that Word within the word unable to speak a word.

To turn back toward sensual youth, bowing to Titians, being beckoned by svelte fräuleins—in short, to subvert the mind to the senses by turning the mind upon sensual history at the final state of decay—would be an escape, a pretense of after-dinner sleep with night very far advanced. But Gerontion rejects (though too late) such pretense as a further deprivation of the consciousness, worthy a Prufrock. Such were a movement in which one could but meet that springing tiger that devours. It is to prolong, through small deliberations, the chilled delirium of the senses. If the word could be spoken by Gerontion, as now it cannot, the word might well be give-sympathize-control. But as Gerontion retires to a sleepy corner, stiffens in his rented house, those unknown words cannot be uttered. The speaker of the poem, then, is our Virgil, but a Virgil speaking with a decayed light of the intellect. Consequently, his vision is only of the inevitable loss of sight, smell, hearing, taste, and touch, in which a materialistic world (which includes us whom Christ's tiger of time inevitably devours) is all too ready to place its trust. He does not speak false visions, tell false fortunes on this subject. He would have us see that truly Claudio's course is not a worthy one:

> For all th' accommodations that thou bear'st
> Are nurs'd by baseness. Thou 'rt by no means valiant;
> For thou dost fear the soft and tender fork
> Of a poor worm: the best of rest is sleep. . . .

We are Claudios, as was Gerontion, and if wise will spurn this loathly worm, Gerontion, that presents itself, thereby ourselves becoming "absolute for death," in something of the manner of Dante in his escape of Hell. For the Word must be pursued bravely within the word it inhabits, within the world. The proper pursuit lies neither in Platonic bypassing of the world's body, nor in a distortion of that body through those perversions by Puritanism which result in Pragmatism, nor in the self-drowning in the blood knowledge of Freudianism. No such romantic distortions of the word will serve to discover the Word. It is, as we have been saying, the danger of romantic distortions of the word that disturbs Eliot in "Prufrock" and "Gerontion" and in his work in general. He is pursuing in these poems that "Giving" which must inevitably cost one "not less than everything," that "complete spiritual freedom" that he speaks of in "Second Thoughts on Humanism."

VII

❦ The form Eliot began to work with is the monologue, not presumed spoken as in Browning, but contained by the mind, a dramatically appropriate attempt upon that faint voice. In Robinson, as we have argued, there is the attempt to dramatize such internal struggles by personifying them and pretending for the personifications an existence external to the mind. There is a similar attempt in Frost, in the representation of male and female which one may take as separate principles in the individual, externalized and particularized for dramatic purposes, the conflict working toward a true marriage, a true wholeness. One may consider "Mending Wall" or "Home Burial" or "West-Running Brook" or even "The Death of the Hired Man" in this light. But one of Eliot's differences from Frost and Robinson is that he knows and chooses to use new ideas about the mind very much in the air at the turn of the century, particularly those ideas concerning phenomenology which led Eliot to study Bradley so closely. Eliot is himself finely attuned to such speculations and more boldly daring in assuming them for poetry's use. To better understand this aspect of Eliot, we need to look rather closely at the early poetry. We may make some general observations initially, in respect to "The Love Song of J. Alfred Prufrock," before we proceed to the implications of Eliot's early position.

The medieval dramatist chose to externalize—that is, personify—aspects of the individual being and play the parts against each other as those parts attempt to dominate the individual being. Though one might consider that Eliot comes to a similar practice as a writer of morality plays after the *Four Quartets*, before the *Quartets* he does not. In "Prufrock" he does not externalize parts, as Robinson and Frost do (and more obviously Yeats in such a medieval poem as his "Dialogue of Self and Soul"), Eliot keeps the parts integral to the individual consciousness, which allows such a fusion as that in "vacant shuttles / Weave the wind." The stage is the internal world. In contrast *Everyman*'s hero is an empty entity, being fought over by that which he is emptied of in the interest of a stylized form—Pride, Anger, Humility, and so on. The play requires an acceptance of its artificiality. But Prufrock on the other hand contains the *I* and *you*, drowned by the I's suicide at the end into a vague identity called "we," a deliberately insidious dissolution. Eliot plays Virgil to the reader's playing Dante in that poem though the guide and spectator do not directly intrude upon the scene as do Dante's two principals. Eliot is in pursuit of a realism in Prufrock whereby he may make the poem a phenomenological exemplum, a point we shall presently consider. As far as the reader's relation to Eliot's poem, however, he is embarked upon a new kind of closet drama, with his own mind containing the mind enacted by the poem. One proof of this point in my own experience is that Eliot's early poetry works most effectively as a private experience, rather than when dramatized by parlor gatherings.

To see Eliot's drama better we might recall two figures of the evening, the one Wordsworth's, the other Eliot's. In doing so, let us recall that Wordsworth's insurmountable problem as poet and as man was a phenomenological one: his constant struggle was to establish the nature of and authenticity of the subjective, and he required for sanity a boldness of action which turned him toward nature as a cause of the mind. We recall the sonnet which begins:

> It is a beauteous evening calm and free
> The holy time is quiet as a Nun
> Breathless with adoration. . . .

It continues, with the kind of bold acceptance of what he suspects in other of his poems as illusion:

to Eliot's poem, we are certain of a coincidence of mind and body. The man lies dying in his bed, and while the illusion of his mind may cause him to confuse the bed clothes with the mortcloth on sculpture, the reader knows the distortion of time and place to be his. In Robinson's "Luke Havergal" there is a little less certainty as to the precise intersection of place and time by a consciousness, but still one rather easily supposes the poem, as we have said, a new soliloquy not intended to divorce the consciousness from time and place as a phenomenological exhibit. Robinson's soliloquy is unlike that which Shakespeare gives Hamlet in that it is the self of Luke Havergal speaking to the self, introspection presented in the third person. It turns in upon the self, where Hamlet's soliloquy, less self-conscious, turns out toward the world as does Wordsworth's sonnet or as Browning's "Soliloquy of a Spanish Cloister." Before Robinson the soliloquy seems to have been a device for unself-conscious revelation of the self. In Robinson it becomes an adaptation of the medieval dialogue whereby the self talks to the self, allowing a dialogue with an immediacy one does not find in the ancient discourses of soul and body.

Prufrock, however, is suspended in a way that Hamlet or the rogue monk in Browning or Luke Havergal are not. Those soliloquies finally touch time and place, have housing in a particular body. Prufrock's does not. It is as if the voice is caught in that illusion that cursed Keats's knight at arms, causing all his woe because he saw nothing all day long, being intoxicated out of time and place by youth itself, which leans sideways to sing its fairy song. Still, although Keats's knight is oblivious of the road traveled, seeing neither before nor after in a fascination of a boundless romantic moment, he is presented as waking older, wiser, sadder. Prufrock never wakes, choosing to see time and place at the poem's end as a drowning.

One can say much of Eliot's poem in explication, and indeed much has been said by a multitude in a multitude of places. But when all is said, the poem remains enigmatic enough to make us consider whether its final nature isn't simply phenomenological. It is the kind of poem Bradleyan arguments call forth. And it is a new separation of art from life, finally, because—though we recognize the Prufrock in ourselves, the cause of our initial fascination, and though we can go far in speculation concerning the psychological causes of this phenomenon—the person of the poem is never resolved in terms of those inevitable limitations of human being, time and place. In a sense the poem and its "person," terms almost interchangeable, are timeless, but it is not a timelessness that satisfies the beholder's mind. However convincing this phenomenon—the poem—it yet lacks that first cause that will allow the mind the satisfaction it requires. At this point Eliot himself is not fully aware of the incompleteness of the phenomenon he presents. Indeed, his critical arguments concerning the necessity of the art object's independence of mind, the necessity of its freedom from the poet's personality, are indications that he has not come to that later insistence that the poem must relate to life. The New Criticism, of which Eliot is often taken to be the father, represents not merely a reaction to old school ways of teaching the poem. It represents a more decided severance of the poem from life than Aristotle's careful separation of poetics from ethics. The effect of that severance has not been as happy as at first supposed: it has separated the reader from the poem in a manner different from that slightly older false separation which took poetry as autobiography. For the mind cannot finally rest in such pure phenomenology as the extremists among the new critics would have poetry be.

Eliot himself was not at rest. There is an uneasiness in him. It is that inevitable uneasiness that one finds a bit before his time in the naturalists, who explained individual existence as an aggregate of accidents. Their more sophisticated successors turn to psychological determinism, as Eliot does in Prufrock. But when one has found out Eliot's buried term to his metaphor, a psychological cause of phenomenology, he is but confirmed in his initial uneasiness. The timelessness of phenomenology has no relation to time. It is a death of the self, finally, which in its horror causes that striking out toward life on the one hand which we generally call existentialism, and the more jolly decay of existential thought on the other which one sees as the basis of the latest religious cult, the God Is Dead phenomenology. This cult, one notices, denies an intersection of timelessness separate from the self located in time and place—that intersection occurring, in Christian thought, with the Advent. Consequently it cannot consider teleological questions, and substitutes for that concern the very vague sociological principles that constitute the community's emotional food. But the substitution of vague Utopianism to satisfy a human demand which cannot be explained by a philosophy is to employ deceit.

This excursion into the thinking of the recent cult is more closely to our point than might at first appear. For in the early Eliot, as represented in "Prufrock," "Gerontion" and other poems of these volumes, the "God Is Dead" mentality is exhibited, out of which Eliot grows toward a larger conception of timelessness, expressed in *Burnt Norton* in particular. The science of the mind that Eliot studied proved insufficient. Phenomenology is after all a development of subjectivity as if it were self-sufficient. What it leads to is a separation of subjective being from any Other. The possibility of any dialogue, that word used so desperately in our time, is doomed. For phenomenology, as that branch of learning had developed by the time of Prufrock, was a heresy to the orthodox family relationship of minds very like the Albigensian in its effective isolation of the individual. So considered, one sees how such a heresy is destructive to the sanity of the artist no less than to other men, for a part of the definition of the artist is that he communicates vision, whether simple simile or complex metaphysical system. The pure application of phenomenology means not only that the poet cannot write for others but that he cannot even write for himself. Schizophrenia is a disease of the self, very much in evidence in the modern world, which argues the dependence of the self upon some other. We begin, that is, to talk to ourselves, the dialogue of the fractured self becoming more and more desperate. It is a kind of rickets of the soul. It is, fortunately, a state of illness from which a return to wholeness is possible, and Prufrock represents just such a point of departure back toward life in the body of Eliot's work, a journey which as we know, leads Eliot to insist finally on the relation of art to life.

VIII

✿ Eliot, as we know from his criticism, does not accept Wordsworth's emotional involvement with nature such as we see revealed in "It Is A Beauteous Evening." Still, he is aware of a decline in the possibility of such involvements on the part of our wasteland world. Prufrock may be taken as an ironic commentary on that inability, directed at a particular inhabitant of the waste land—the intellectually acute, cultured resident who inhabits the never-never land which Dante named Ante-Hell. Another kind of inhabitant of the Ante-Hell is represented by Sweeney. If we look at "Sweeney Erect," we see that Eliot's epigraph, rather than acting as a note on where the reader is supposed to imagine himself, as in "Prufrock," actually sets up as a foil to Sweeney's world the lost world still possible to Wordsworth, a world in which the sensibilities of the individual might at least relate themselves emotionally to the natural world. He does so by casting Sweeney's mate against the deserted Aspatia. It is a desperate falling off, even from the romantic view, but it represents a movement back toward the world of time from the spectacle "Prufrock" represents.

In "Sweeney among the Nightingales" the same sort of contrast is set up, with the difference being that the contrast centers more upon Sweeney than on the mate he is taken with at the moment. The epigram functions as it does in "Sweeney Erect," the cry of the slain hero, Agamemnon, serving to signify the small sordid world Sweeney inhabits in contrast. There is a strong hint that Sweeney too will be done in, but his will be an insignificant death. Agamemnon, while no large mind such as one has in Oedipus, is engaged in his world in such a way that his death can disturb the universe, as Sweeney's won't. All the instruments of the poem agree on Sweeney's imminent demise. Veil the constellations with impending doom, hush the seas for the awful moment. So what? For Sweeney is what a Prufrock wishes himself. Pithecanthropos erectus isn't so far removed from a pair of ragged claws as from Prufrock. Little consolation, for as Prufrock would know, he himself is less far removed from Jocasta than from Oedipus. But even so, once more there is some indication of an attempt to draw figures toward a relation to time. Eliot's point of view itself in the Sweeney poems suggests a concern for a significant life larger than the self.

To enact the body of Eliot's poetry by a careful reading, then, is to experience a steady spiritual growth. It is, clearly enough, Eliot's own development which is unfolded, though he disguises his "personality." Disguise is the principal purpose of such an essay as "Tradition and the Individual Talent," an essay whose distinctions are not finally convincing since they are not so to Eliot, who is in that essay the romantic in flight from romanticism. And even as Dante intended the *Comedy* to lead those astray back to the true way, so Eliot sees such a use of his own poetry, a purpose which becomes increasingly overt as he becomes surer of the road he is embarked upon. Very soon he moves beyond a concern for Bradleyan presentation of a state of mind, not abandoning psychological realism, but taking it as a point from which to enlarge upon spiritual realism. So Eliot becomes for us a new Everyman, whom many have found personally satisfying in leading to a view of life, though far more have found him satisfying as a subject to talk about or explicate. That is, he is a favorite substitute for Michelangelo at cocktail parties.

Perhaps those open preachings of Wordsworth about nature's healing powers, the longings of Keats, and the implied longings of Browning may be less effective, either as drama or as instruction, than the forgetting of ourselves into a consciousness on its quest, whether Prufrock's or Tiresias'. We become the Prufrock we are, cowardly in ignoring cowardliness; we become a larger self in the consciousness of Gerontion, who meets us honestly upon this question of spiritual failure in the light of history (though it seems the *dark* of history to him, he being blind in a way that brings none of Oedipus' inner light). We move through *The Waste Land* toward a concern for, and dream of, life-giving waters. We prepare through the ritual of *Ash Wednesday* to imbibe Dante's high rivers, Lethe and Eunoe, and in consequence are prepared to move on beyond time in the *Four Quartets*. That move is possible—the move out of time—only since Eliot himself has come to terms with time, a coming to terms that makes it possible for him to abide that unreal city, London, working at editorial duties with Faber & Faber. For the spiritual development in Eliot's poetry is not a pre-conceived strategem, unfolded gradually to take in the gullible, as Karl Shapiro would have it. It is, again I insist, a very real development in Eliot, in which he risked himself. That is why his credentials as a reader's Virgil are honorable. For Eliot's poetry is no fictional fairy tale nor romance. He came firmly to rest on a rock of ancient deposit in the world, as he tells us in *The Rock:*

> . . . the Son of Man was not crucified once for all,
> The blood of the Martyrs not shed once for all,
> The lives of the Saints not given once for all:
> But the Son of Man is crucified always
> And there shall be Martyrs and Saints.
> And if blood of Martyrs is to flow on the steps
> We must first build the steps;
> And if the Temple is to be cast down
> We must first build the Temple.

Eliot's is a position that reconciles itself to the endlessness of worldly failure and grief, as E. A. Robinson could not. Robinson never was able to move beyond pity and fear, out of hell, as Dante and Eliot were able to do. That is why he continues to wrestle important questions in a poetry that is largely rhetorical prose, in "Zola," in "The Man Who Died Twice," in the "Man Against the Sky." That is why he can cry out with pathos, the old cry in the night

> . . . after nineteen hundred years the shame
> Still clings. . . .
> Tell me, O Lord—tell me, O Lord, how long
> Are we to keep Christ writhing on the cross!

Eliot has made popular several critical phrases, among them the now-notorious "objective correlative." It is a literary term as we use it, concerned with the artist's objectifying the world of art toward excluding personality from art. Initially, it was a theory necessary as a corollary to Eliot's phenomenological concern, to the suspending of the art object with its anchor in reality, in the eye of the beholder. We see the method Eliot means by the term in Prufrock's *teacups, coffee spoons, dooryards.* Images, situations, which allow emotional response to arise out of the object or circumstances. It is an attempt to make the poem *be,* in MacLeish's word for it, rather than *mean.* It is a concern for making the poem dramatic, so persuasively so that one is enabled by the poem itself to suspend his disbelief, enter into the poem with his own emotional life. But we would make a mistake to suppose that Eliot intends the experience to be only entertainment of the reader's emotions and an exercise for his wit. Even in that carefully guarded essay "Tradition and the Individual Talent," he is interested in *"significant* emotion."* He means for one to be so enlivened that as a result of the poem he must change his life. It is in this manner that Eliot understands poetry to relate to life. Reading Eliot's poetry as he thinks it may be read is to experience a spiritual journey that is immediately personal to the reader, since it is his own journey, even though his disbelief return out of suspension. It reveals as well the particular mind of Eliot, since the journey undertaken furnishes not simply materials of personal experience turned to art but attaches to the "significant emotion" that relate themselves to life. And yet, there is an enactment of the journey of the Western mind itself, elements of which are reflected by the allusions of "Gerontion" and *The Waste Land* in particular. We have presented, in effect, a dramatic allegory about the spiritual quest of Everyman and Every-civilization. The disembodied consciousness becomes the stage wherein (not whereon) we meet ourselves in an experience which is a literary equivalent of the biologist's metaphor so thoroughly explored since Sir Charles Lyell and Charles Darwin: ontogeny recapitulates phylogeny. The poetry works toward a relation of the history of an individual's spiritual development to the history of the development of that society of which he is the latest example. In Eliot this metaphor is first in terms of psychology, or phenomenology, which is then enlarged to theology in that it incorporates first and final causes in the pursuit of timelessness. Hence those words from *The Rock*, the words which indicate the relation of a soul whose earthly identity we address as Thomas Stearns Eliot to that inclusive Being that intersected history some two thousand years ago. For if the question of *being* itself, the very possibility of the existence of the self, came so sharply into question, leading to Maritain and to Sartre, and eventually to the latest American Billy Sunday of the intelligentsia, Thomas J. J. Altizer, Eliot himself was neither reduced to desperate action nor philosophical fumbling. He set about finding a relation of causes larger than those satisfied by the phenomenological. History, he discovered, is overcome by the individual soul, in Eliot's view, when it realizes that "the Son of Man was not crucified once for all." That is to have finally arrived at that position, after exploring history,

> And know the place for the first time.
> Through the unknown, remembered gate
> Quick now, here, now, always—
> A condition of complete simplicity
> (Costing no less than everything)
> And all shall be well and
> All manner of thing shall be well
> When the tongues of flame are in-folded
> Into the crowned knots of fire
> And the fire and the rose are one.

After such a vision, even Prufrock can go through the remembered gate and into *The Cocktail Party*, a work incorporating a much larger world than the old tea-party we read about in 1917. Now not only is he reconciled to the trivial bald spot in his hair and the easy talk of "you and me" but reconciled as well to Celia, who, in the midst of pestilence at her missionary outpost, is crucified on an ant-hill. But the final shocking reconciliation is, as we see it, carried in Celia's lover, who comes to see that his choice is right, though quite different from Celia's and at first sight seemingly unheroic. Eliot writes his "comedy" as he calls it, pointing out in the person of Peter Quilpe, the necessity of the individual's discovery of health in relation to his own being, not as measured by the history of martyrdom, by stones or on ant hills. Peter goes on about his movie-making, as Eliot about his publishing, accepting Celia's death, as Eliot accepts Pound's on his ant hill at Pisa or St. Elizabeths, knowing the possibility of less sensational sacrifice. Perhaps Celia and Pound, but few of their tortured followers or detractors, see with Eliot's calm eye how "All manner of thing shall be well." That Pound does is hinted by that moving small paragraph tribute amidst the long essays and memoirs of the special Eliot issue of the *Sewanee Review*. Pound writes, recalling the old days, "Who is there now for me to share a joke with?" *Joke*. Larger than the implication of humor or wit. Just as Eliot's own distinction between the romantic and classical mind is larger than literary, as both Eliot and Pound know after the terrors of sedate London existence and the exhilarating experience of the cage at Pisa. Eliot said, we recall,

> The romantic is deficient or undeveloped in his ability
> to distinguish between fact and fancy, whereas the
> classicist, or adult mind, is thoroughly realist—
> without illusions, without daydreams, without hope, without
> bitterness, and with an abundance of resignation.

Eliot's poetry is, finally, an enlargement from a romantic to a classical state. It is a development in which the emphasis is shifted from the spectacular appearance to the subtle implication. That such a shift in itself destroys poetry's power can be entertained only by one who takes the power of *Oedipus the King* to reside in murder, incest, suicide, and physical blindness.